St Cuthbert's Way

A PILGRIMS' COMPANION

St Cuthbert's Way

A PILGRIMS' COMPANION

by

MARY LOW

with illustrations by Dick Warren

WILD GOOSE PUBLICATIONS

For Bruce
and for
all the young people,
past, present and future
of High Cross, St Cuthbert's
Melrose

Now my wee book, whate'er betide
Thou e'en maun face the warld wide;
The Forest, Tiviotdale and the Merse
Thro thae, at least, thou maun traverse;
Dink'd up in hamely russet claes
Thou now must face thy freends and faes
But oh, may never critic rude
Stretch forth his hands to shed thy blude...
But if for little rompish laits
I hear that thou a pandy gets
Wi patience thou maun bear the brunt
An e'en put up wi mony a dunt.

Andrew Scott of Bowden

Contents

Foreword

It was a great joy to be asked to write a foreword for this book. It evoked so many memories. I recall that my father taught for his whole career at St Cuthbert's Grammar School, Newcastle-on-Tyne, where the school song opened with the words

> *By the banks of silvery Wear,*
> *'neath proud Dunelm's towered shrine,*
> *rests the body of our patron*
> *hard by Beda[1], sage divine.*

This my sisters and I sang along with enthusiastically – although we did not attend the school itself.[2] Cuthbert's memory was a vibrant part of my childhood. I cannot forget the first time I saw the Holy Island of Lindisfarne – the end point of the pilgrimage described in this book. The element of danger stands out in my mind: would we beat the tide across the causeway, as the silver ribbons of water crept almost imperceptibly across the golden sands? The pilgrims' refuge stood out on the causeway as a cautionary tale: they had left it too late. Cuthbert caught our imagination as we too crept over the rocks to the tiny islet, St Cuthbert's island, and searched for the tiny black beads, St Cuthbert's beads.

Here, we were told, he first sought solitude. I could understand this: in my first attempts at seeking space away from my family – I was 14 years old – even I could cope with a few hours in the rain and wind on that lonely spot. But at night, looking out through the darkening skies to the flashing lighthouse of the Inner Farne island, I realised that his search for solitude with God was far deeper than any of my feeble imitations.

This was years before St Cuthbert's Way became well known. But my early wanderings around Northumbria and the enchantment that Cuthbert, Aidan, Oswald and Hilda have for me give an inkling that these ancient roots, these connections between land and faith, remain a rich source for exploration. They also offer a resource for today's spiritual quest. What Mary Low's book does is to give a rich context for one specific pilgrimage, and in a way accessible to pilgrims of all faiths and those beyond faith. She connects St Cuthbert's Way pilgrimage with the searching and yearning common to all humanity. We are told that to embark on a pilgrimage journey is part of the wellsprings of many religions. For Christianity it was the journey of the Wise Men that culminated in the vision of the child of Peace. Russian Christianity sees that journey continuing in the Babushka's Christmas gift-giving to poor children of her neighbourhood.[3] Jesus himself went on regular pilgrimages to the Holy City of Jerusalem. For Islam, the focus of pilgrimage is Mecca. It is a timely moment to show how pilgrimage can meet a deep human need, when it is so easy for deeper yearnings to be stifled by cultural pressures to spend, to 'shop till we drop'. The words of Peter Millar, former warden of Iona Abbey, will always ring in my ears: 'Have you still room in your life to be a pilgrim?'[4]

Mary Low connects walking St Cuthbert's Way with ecological sensitivity. (And she is already well known for her work in the field of the Celtic love of nature).[5] Joy in the Divine revealed through the creatures of earth, sky and sea was common to the early Celtic and Anglo-Saxon saints – as well as found in sacred scripture. At a time of severe crisis in the environment, walking the way can make real for the wayfarer the sacredness of water (Holy Wells form an important part), of trees, of the struggles of monks and poor farmers to sow and harvest their crops and the kindness they display in dealing with birds and animals. A kindness which is of course reciprocated – as in the much-loved story of the furry sea otters who came to lick Cuthbert's feet dry after he had spent the night in prayer in the icy waters of the North Sea.

These lives of Cuthbert, his contemporaries and forebears are told simply, using early primary sources. Maybe some of them are well known – but their power still holds! As the reader might expect, Mary Low is a good storyteller: for example, when describing the tragic slaughter of the battle of Flodden Field, she writes:

> *If there are tears in heaven Cuthbert must surely have shed them that day as 40,000 men from north and south of the Border laid into each other with guns and pikes. Casualties were so heavy that, as night fell, neither side was sure who had won. (p. 134–5)*

This is just one example where grief over slaughter of the past reminds us that in all these years humanity seems never to let go of its love affair with war.

Through the story of Cuthbert we are linked with Iona's story and with Brigit of Ireland. But not only are we given a history of the saints – as befits a pilgrimage – but also a feast of legend, folk-lore and local song, always with a health warning that all is not always what it seems!

St Cuthbert's Way: A Pilgrims' Companion is at the same time extremely practical. Mary Low is concerned for wheelchair users, those not so goat-footed, and the discomfort where no toilets are available. (My own experiences in the desert of Rajasthan come to mind...) We are also given a range of inspiring resources in the form of readings and songs – as a different form of food for the journey.

But, when all is said and done, the proof of the pudding is in the eating. Walking St Cuthbert's Way may be simply a holiday in beautiful countryside; it may be a discovery of the fascination of Celtic/Anglian Northumbria; or it may be a pilgrimage which brings more questions than it provides answers. But then, that is the only path to wisdom.

Mary Grey
Editor of *Ecotheology* magazine

1   Beda is St Bede, one of the most important resources for this book. 'Hard by' means near. Dunelm is, of course, the old name for Durham.

2   It was – and is – a boys' school!

3   Babushka is the old grandmother. The story relates that she was too old and tired, and the night was too cold for her to accompany the Wise Men in their search.

4   This was summer 1998, when I was on the island leading a group.

5   See Mary Low, *Celtic Christianity and Nature*, Edinburgh: Edinburgh University Press, 1996.

Introduction

In the steps of St Cuthbert?

St Cuthbert's Way is not an ancient pilgrim route, but parts of it were probably walked by pilgrims in the past, and other parts would certainly have been known to Cuthbert and his contemporaries. From the seventh till the ninth century, visitors would have come and gone regularly between Lindisfarne and its daughter-house at Melrose, either on business or on pilgrimage. Cuthbert would have known the area intimately, from his childhood and from his pastoral journeys. He was a great walker: he had to be. There were very few roads here in the seventh century and it was easier to walk or ride than to bump along in a cart. The countryside was criss-crossed by a network of footpaths and bridle-ways and these are what Cuthbert would have used. We know that he could ride and sometimes he went on horseback, but more often he did the rounds of the villages on foot.[1] Sometimes he would be away for a week, a fortnight, even a month at a time, living with the 'rough hill folk'. Bede tells us that he made a point of searching out 'those steep rugged places in the hills which other preachers dreaded to visit because of their poverty and squalor'.[2] If he were alive today, he would probably visit people in towns and cities as well, but he knew from experience that beautiful scenery is no protection against hardship and he made it his business to understand and encourage people, especially if they were isolated or in trouble.

Where exactly did he go? We can only guess, but 'steep rugged places' within a day's walk of Melrose would include the southern slopes of the Lammermuirs and the Leader valley, the Black Hill at Earlston, the Eildons, Teviotdale and the hills around Hawick, and above all the great mass of the Cheviots. From his days as Prior of Lindisfarne, he would also have known the Northumberland coast, parts of Berwickshire and the hills inland towards Wooler. As bishop, he travelled even further afield (p.47).

No one knows exactly which route he took between Melrose and Lindisfarne. Sometimes he travelled by boat. The rivers Leader, Tweed and Teviot are all mentioned in his early Lives. On one occasion, after several years living at Old Melrose, we are told that he 'sailed away' privately and secretly.[3] This can only mean that he sailed down the Tweed. On another occasion, he sailed from Old Melrose to the territory of the Picts and got caught in a storm along the way.[4] The nearest Pictish communities of any size were in Fife, with some in Lothian, so he probably travelled downstream as far as Tweedmouth, then north, along the coast, past Coldingham and Dunbar. For visiting the hill-folk however, he can only have gone on foot. It's impossible to imagine him not using Dere Street, the old Roman road. It was the only reasonable road in the area and ran very close to Old Melrose. From Dere Street, he would have branched off onto larger pathways, sometimes along the river valleys and finally onto mountain tracks.

In the end, I don't think it matters very much where he walked. Cuthbert himself would probably have been bemused that anyone should want to follow in his footsteps literally, like the page-boy in Good King Wenceslas. If anyone had asked Cuthbert about his 'way' he might have said that he did not have one, not one of his own. He did, however, have a way of life, the way of Jesus of Nazareth, and if he is listening from his place in heaven, he is probably delighted to know that people still want to follow that way, a way of faith and compassion.

What you can expect from this book

The *Companion* is divided into four main sections: 'Cuthbert and his Contemporaries' (1) sets the scene, introducing the main personalities and events. It describes Cuthbert's childhood and youth, the troubled background, the coming of Christianity, the time of crisis and change following the Synod of Whitby, his life as prior, hermit and bishop and the beginnings of the pilgrimage to his tomb.

The Field Guide (2) opens out into a much broader view. It takes you step by step along St Cuthbert's Way, introducing a whole range of subjects and places of interest, from pre-history to the present. It focuses mainly, but not exclusively, on subjects which are likely to be of interest to a pilgrim. There is more about Cuthbert and his contemporaries, but you will also find mention of pre-Christian Roman and Celtic religion as well as later Christian traditions: the rise and fall of the Border abbeys, Michael Scot, Duns Scotus, the Covenanters, Gypsies and the Kirk, Scotland's first deaconess, the 'scandalous' life of Josephine Butler and how a future pope spent the night with about a hundred women just outside Berwick. There was once an old Irish tradition of *Dindshenchas* or Place-Lore: stories about features of the landscape and the people who lived there. The *Companion* is a bit like that but it is also a Companion for the present, for what is happening here and now in this part of the country.

'Going on a Pilgrimage' (3) looks at the persistence of pilgrimage through the ages. We hear of the reckless and extraordinary faith of people deliberately setting off into the unknown with no idea where they were going; others who went on pilgrimage as a penance, in search of healing or simply for the love of God. We hear of the unholy scams of the late-medieval pilgrimage industry and the reforms which followed. We hear from St Samthann of Clonbroney, the eighth century Irish abbess who thought pilgrimages were a waste of time – for some people at least; and finally, we look at the survival of pilgrimage and its revival in the present.

The Resources section (4) offers a collection of readings, songs and prayers for people to use and enjoy along the way. There are extracts from the earliest known writings about Cuthbert, Boisil, Aidan and some of the people they encountered. There are also Bible readings, poems and meditations from later Christian writers and a small number of readings from non-Christian traditions as well.

There is also a small but very useful section called 'Before You Go'. This is full of practical information about how to plan your pilgrimage, where to get information, where to stay, what to take and so on. It follows immediately after this introduction. If you are travelling in a big group you will already know how important it is to plan ahead. This is particularly the case for Holy Island where the sheer volume of visitors sometimes puts a serious strain on the island's resources. There are always quiet places waiting to be discovered, but finding somewhere for larger groups to meet, eat, celebrate etc. in the area around the Priory and the village can be a bit of a nightmare unless you have made arrangements ahead of time. Don't worry about this if there are just a few of you, or if you are by yourself. But Lindisfarne is a tidal island and everyone should plan around that.

What the Companion does not include

There is far more to be said about St Cuthbert's Way than could possibly be fitted into one pocket-sized book. In trying to imagine what pilgrims would be most interested in, I have had to make some difficult choices. I would like to have said more about nature and the environment, geology, agriculture and what it's like to live in Northumberland and the Borders now. I have said nothing about King Arthur (although there are some local Arthurian legends) and very little about Sir Walter Scott. Surprisingly, perhaps, you won't find much theology either. I had intended to include more but decided that the role of the *Companion* is to provide starting-points for reflection. I have assumed that Christian pilgrims are interested in more than just 'churchy' subjects and in outlooks and religions other than their own.

The *Companion* is not just for religious people. It assumes an interest in and an openness towards Christianity, but it is also for seekers and searchers – people like Jennifer Lash whose refreshingly honest *On Pilgrimage* challenges and encourages modern pilgrims of whatever background.[5] Many – perhaps most – of the best things about St Cuthbert's Way won't be described in this

book: 'There is a time to keep silence and a time to speak.' For
long stretches, the field-guide says nothing at all, leaving you open
to whatever is going on and free to discover the meaning of your
own pilgrimage for yourself.

Notes

1   Passim
2   Bede, *Life of Cuthbert*, 9. He made similar journeys in Northumberland. ibid. 16.
3   Anonymous *Life of Cuthbert* 3.1.
4   Anon. 2.4.
5   Jennifer Lash, *On Pilgrimage*, London, 1998.

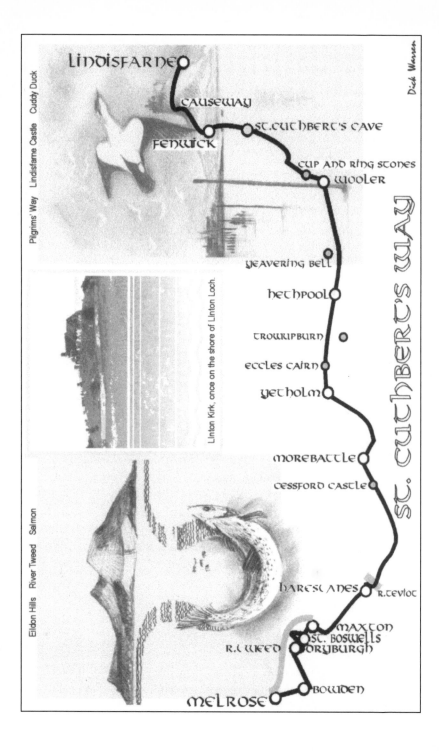

ST. CUTHBERT'S WAY

Dick Warren

Pilgrims' Way   Lindisfarne Castle   Cuddy Duck

LINDISFARNE
CAUSEWAY
FENWICK
ST. CUTHBERT'S CAVE
CUP AND RING STONES
WOOLER
YEAVERING BELL
HETHPOOL
TROWUPBURN
ECCLES CAIRN
YETHOLM
MOREBATTLE
CESSFORD CASTLE
HARESTANES
R.TEVIOT
MAXTON
ST. BOSWELLS
R.TWEED   DRYBURGH
BOWDEN
MELROSE

Linton Kirk, once on the shore of Linton Loch.

Eildon Hills   River Tweed   Salmon

Before you go
(Practicalities)

First Stop

Detailed information about the route, accommodation, baggage service etc. is available all the year round from the two Tourist Information Centres (TICs) listed below. They also sell guides, maps etc. If you are sending for any of these, please include postage and packing.

✤ Scottish Borders Tourist Information Centre, Murray's Green, Jedburgh, TD8 6BE, Scotland. Tel 01835 863170; Fax 01835 864099; e-mail – sbtb@scotborders.co.uk

✤ Tourist Information Centre, The Maltings, Eastern Lane, Berwick-upon-Tweed, TD15 1DT, England. Phone – 01289 330733; Fax – 01289 330448.

Other TICs in the Scottish Borders carry the same information, Easter–October only, and some of the merchandise. Another useful contact for information is:

Countryside Ranger Service, Harestanes Visitor Centre, Ancrum, Jedburgh, TD8 6UQ. Phone 01835 830281.

How long does it take?

That's entirely up to you. The distance is just over 62 miles/100km. The walk was originally presented in four stages but this is no longer the case and people generally make their own timetable. One man ran the entire distance in a day. Scotwalk, the holiday company, do it in nine. Some people do it a stage at a time over several months. Whatever you decide, be aware that there are some interesting diversions along the route.You might also like to spend some time in and around Melrose at the beginning, make a half-day excursion to Scott's View overlooking Old Melrose (p. 59) or spend an extra day on Holy Island at the end.

Can I do the route in either direction?

Yes. You can start in Holy Island and end up in Melrose if you like. The way-markers can be read in either direction. The *Companion* works best with Holy Island at the end, but Melrose was once a pilgrimage centre too.

Route-finders and guide books

St Cuthbert's Way: a Pilgrims' Companion is designed to be used in conjunction with a route-finder such as:

 St Cuthbert's Way: summary guide book by Roger Smith and Ron Shaw. Price £1.50. From TICs.

This is a good-sized leaflet rather than a book. It won't weigh you down and gives practical instructions ('turn right and then first left... ') and some background information. Also sketch maps – but you will need at least one detailed map as well. If you have room in your back-pack for another book, the official trail guide is an expanded version of the above:

 St Cuthbert's Way: official trail guide by Roger Smith and Ron Shaw, published by The Stationery Office, Edinburgh, 1997, price £12.99. Available from TICs, locally in bookshops and to order elsewhere.

The trail guide overlaps with the *Companion* in some places but it also covers more general subjects which there has not been room for here. It includes a strip map (scale 1: 40,000) of the whole walk, a long narrow view of it, divided into sections. This makes it possible to have everything on one sheet but won't let you get your bearings on more distant features like hills etc. See Maps (below).

 There is also a small introductory leaflet called simply 'St Cuthbert's Way'. It is available free from TICs. It should not be used to follow the route on the ground but is useful for an overview at the planning stage and for reference.

Accommodation and Facilities Guide
Essential leaflet, available free from TICs. Lists all youth-hostels, campsites, B&Bs, guesthouses and hotels along the route. Also shops, pubs, cafés, toilets, public phones, health centres, chemists, opening times of visitor attractions and all kinds of other useful information. Accommodation can fill up quickly, especially in summer and on holiday weekends, so it's as well to book ahead if at all possible. The TIC in Jedburgh will book all your accommodation for you if you like, at no extra charge.

Getting there by public transport
The main London–Edinburgh rail-link stops at Berwick. There are bus and coach services to Melrose (and other parts of St Cuthbert's Way) from there. The Glasgow–London intercity route stops at Carlisle and there is a bus service from there to Galashiels, just two miles from Melrose. The Accommodation and Facilities Guide (above) has contact numbers for time-table information.

Walking holidays / guided walks
Several companies now offer organised walking holidays along St Cuthbert's Way.

 Scotwalk Ltd is based locally and featured in 1998 on the

BBC's Holiday Programme. Their address is Traquair Mill House, Innerleithen, Peeblesshire, EH44 6PT. Phone 01896 830515. Fax 01896 830889. Website: www.scotwalk.co.uk

Others include:

⊕ Avalon Trekking Scotland, near Perth (10738 624194)

⊕ C'n'Do Scotland Ltd, Stirling (01786 445703)

⊕ Easyways, Falkirk (01324 714132)

⊕ Sherpa Expeditions, Hounslow (0181 577 2717)

Guided walks, led by the countryside ranger service, take place regularly along sections of the route. For more information on any of the above, see Accommodation and Facilities Guide.

Carry-Lite: door-to-door baggage transfer

Whose brilliant idea was this? Instead of lugging a back-pack around for over 60 miles, you can now arrange for Carry-lite to carry it for you. They will collect your luggage from your overnight accommodation and deliver it to wherever you are going. You do have to pay for it (£25 for 5 days, per item up to 40lbs/18kgs, or £7 per day) but you may think it's worth it. It's best to book ahead and this qualifies you for a discount, but they may be able to fit you in at short notice as well. Leaflet available from TICs or phone 01665 575767 or mobile 0976 356459.

Level of fitness and experience

There are low-level and hilly stretches of St Cuthbert's Way. Parts of it can be unexpectedly demanding so you do need to be reasonably fit. You should also know how to use a map and compass. The path is way-marked throughout, but parts of it can be tricky, especially in the Cheviots in poor weather.

Pilgrims with disabilities

Sadly, most of St Cuthbert's Way is presently inaccessible to people with disabilities. The Companion includes access information for some places along the route (e.g. Melrose Abbey, Dryburgh Abbey, Wooler Common, Lindisfarne) but it has not been possible to complete a full survey. Given the terrain, it's difficult to imagine how the whole route could ever be fully accessible, but it is possible to get to parts of it and more research may broaden the options. If you find a stretch of the route which you think might be accessible, either for wheelchair-users or for people who can walk up to 1 mile, please let me know and, if possible, complete an access survey form (at end of book). Send the information to me, Mary Low, c/o Wild Goose Publications, Unit 16, Six Harmony Row, Glasgow G51 3BA. Feel free to photocopy the form as required. All distances given in the access sections are approximate. Some of the supposedly accessible toilets along the route are kept locked to avoid vandalism. This can be distressing, but the answer is to get your own Radar key and bring it with you. One key fits all. They cost about £2.50 and are available direct from Radar, 25 Mortimer Street, London, W1N 8AB. Phone 0171 637 5400. You have to confirm in writing that you are a disabled person.

Maps
Although there are signposts all along the route and sketch maps in the Summary Guide Book, it is essential to have at least one good large-scale map such as:

 Harvey's Walkers' Map. All of St Cuthbert's Way on one sheet. £6.95 from TICs and some bookshops (similar map included with the official trail guide)

 Ordnance Survey Landranger Series, sheets 73, 74 and 75. Scale 1:50,000. £5.25 from TICs, bookshops and outdoor activities shops. Means carrying three maps but makes it easier to see where you are in relation to other places.

Use of Melrose Abbey and Lindisfarne Priory
Both of these beautiful old ruins are open to visitors during the day. Normally there is an admission charge but if you want to use either of them for a religious service, say, at the beginning or the end of your pilgrimage, you should be able to get in free if you plan ahead. For Melrose Abbey, you should apply in writing, well in advance, to Historic Scotland, Longmore House, Salisbury Place, Edinburgh, EH9 1SH. For Lindisfarne Priory write to: Northern

Regional Office, English Heritage, Bessie Surtees House, 42 Sandhill, Newcastle, NE1 3JS.

What to take

Good boots (not brand new ones) or other suitable footwear. Waterproofs. Warm clothes. Maps, guides etc. Plenty to eat and drink (some parts of the route have no facilities at all). In medieval times, pilgrims carried a staff. This is not just a quaint idea. Some of the paths are steep and/or slippery so a stick or walking pole is worth considering.

Safe crossing times to Holy Island

It's very important to plan your route so as to arrive at Holy Island when the tide is out and the causeway or the sands are safe for crossing. Information about tides is available from:

 Berwick-upon-Tweed Tourist Information Centre (see above)

 Wooler Tourist Information Centre (posted on door when closed, April–October)

 Holy Island Post Office, Marygate, Holy Island, TD15 2SD, phone – 01289 389271

The tide varies slightly with weather conditions so advance information can only ever be approximate. There are two ways to cross to the island: either by the causeway or by the traditional pilgrims' path across the sands. The pilgrims' path brings you in closer to the village but it is covered by water for at least one hour longer (before and after high tide) than the causeway, so only use it if you are sure you have plenty of time. Both routes have a refuge box for emergencies but that does not make it worth the risk. The currents are dangerous and the refuge boxes cold and uncomfortable.

If you need to stay overnight while waiting, there is a campsite at Goswick, two miles north of the causeway along a coastal path, a B&B at Fenwick and another at Beal where there is also an Expedition Centre with dormitory-type accommodation (see Accommodation and Facilities Guide) If you're not staying on the island overnight make sure you allow plenty of time to cross back again later. Camping on Holy Island is strictly prohibited but there are some B&Bs and hotels.

Holy Island minibus

This could be useful if you don't want to have to rush back because of the tides, or if you just feel you've walked far enough! For bookings and information, contact J.H Douglas, 4 Crossgates, Holy Island, TD15 2ST. Phone 01289 389236.

Use of churches, halls etc. on Holy Island

All three churches on Holy Island are kept open most of the time for prayer and for the use of islanders, pilgrims and tourists. It's not usually necessary to get special permission for individuals and very small groups simply to look around or sit for a while, as long as you're prepared to fit in. Larger groups should make inquiries first, especially if you intend to hold any kind of talk or liturgy. If in doubt, check. Details below.

✤ St Mary's Church (Anglican) is open to visitors during the day. It is also a working parish church with its own daily round of activities. Out of courtesy, and to avoid arriving in the middle of some other event, please write in advance to: The Vicarage, Holy Island, TD15 2RX.

✤ St Mary's Churchyard, including the area around the statue of St Aidan. As above.

✤ St Aidan's Church (Catholic) is open most days but also has its own programme of events, especially on Saturdays in summer. To make sure it's open and to avoid clashing with other groups, phone Andy and Anna Raine on 01289 389351. Phone bookings preferred, but you can also write to them at 'Settled', 3 Lilburn Terrace, Holy Island, TD15 2SA. If you get no reply after several calls, the parish priest in Seahouses (01665 720427) may be able to help.

✤ St Cuthbert's Church (United Reformed) is now a Christian visitor centre and is open most of the time with displays, suggestions for walks and a steward on hand for information. It also has tea and coffee-making facilities and toilets, including one for people with disabilities. The centre can be hired by the hour (prices on application) and can also provide speakers and worship-leaders if required. The address for bookings is: Revd Ian Fosten, The Manse, Holy Island, TD15 2SB.

 The Village Hall. This is also available for hire during the day. It costs roughly £20 for 2 hours or £40 for the day, holds 100–120 people and has a stage and a kitchen. Bookings to: The Development Officer, North View, Marygate, Holy Island.

Churches along St Cuthbert's Way
There are plans to produce a booklet with times of church services on or near St Cuthbert's Way. Look out for it, if you want to time your journey accordingly.

Every effort has been made to ensure that the details and descriptions given in this book are correct, but neither the author nor the publisher can accept any liability for loss, damage or injury incurred as a result of any part of the book.

St Cuthbert and his contemporaries

One morning in the year 651, a group of monks were standing by the gates of their monastery on the banks of the Tweed. They had recently had news of the death of Aidan, the monk of Iona who had come to the Borders as a missionary 16 years previously. He had been the founder of their mother-house in Lindisfarne and they must have wondered how they were going to manage without him. Their own abbot was away so they could not discuss it with him. The sound of hoof-beats drew their attention. A messenger, perhaps? He looked very young. The boy dismounted and, without speaking, gave his horse and spear to a servant and went into the church. One monk turned to another and said: 'Behold the servant of the Lord.' It was a moment they would remember later. When the boy came out, the same monk welcomed him and asked why he had come. 'To leave the world behind,' said the boy.[1] For the rest of his life, Cuthbert would always be wanting to leave the world behind, and always he would be drawn back into it. The old monk who welcomed him was Boisil. The monastery was Old Melrose.

This story comes to us from the Venerable Bede who got it from a young monk who was standing next to Boisil that day. His name was Sigfrith and most of what we know about Cuthbert comes from people like him. Some memories were collected and written down at the end of the seventh century, about ten years after Cuthbert's death, by a monk of Lindisfarne who does not tell us his own name. He is known simply as 'the Anonymous'. Later, Bede wrote a long poem about Cuthbert's life and, in the 720s, a prose Life with stories never included before, by people who had known Cuthbert in their youth.[2]

Childhood and growing up

No one knows exactly where Cuthbert was born, but he was conceived in troubled times. The British chieftain Cadwalla invaded the Borders in AD 633 and there was a year of burning and pillaging before he was driven back. Cuthbert was born the following year. That, at least, is the traditional date, but we know nothing about his birth or even who his parents were. He has an Anglian name and was brought up in the Anglian community, that is, among the Germanic settlers who had moved into eastern England and south-east Scotland during the fifth and sixth centuries. They were as well-established here as most Americans are in the USA but the native Britons were still resentful of them sometimes, though they lived as neighbours. Cuthbert's birth also coincided, within a few months, with the arrival of the Iona mission, led by St Aidan. The child would have grown up hearing about this Irish exile, this guru from a different culture and people, who brought them the Gospel of Jesus in broken English.

When he was eight years old, Cuthbert went to live with a young woman called Kenswith as her foster-son.[3] This need not mean that he was an orphan. In Ireland and Scandinavia, probably in England too, noble families often sent their sons to be fostered by other noble families and sometimes by the Church.[4] Kenswith is described as *sanctimonialis vidua* – a widow living a consecrated life. She was still alive when the anonymous Life was written around AD 700. We are not told how old she was by then, but unless she was over eighty, she must have been a young widow, barely into her twenties, when she fostered Cuthbert. It's odd that neither his mother nor his father enters the story, even for a moment. That he was not altogether poor is suggested by the fact that as a young man he rode a horse and carried a spear; but he also worked as a shepherd for a while: not generally the occupation of choice for a young nobleman.[5]

Kenswith lived at a place called Hruringaham.[6] Some people think this was near Wooler (p.131); others, that it was near Old Melrose. In 1930, the Berwickshire Naturalists' Club organised an outing to Brotherstone farm near Smailholm, where Rev. W. L. Sime pointed out a row of ancient ash trees. This, he said, was the site of the ancient village of Wrangholm, alias Hruringaham. Wrangholm is marked on Armstrong's map of 1771, but I have not been able to trace it back further than that.[7] Brotherstone is just three miles from Old Melrose; Channelkirk, 16 miles away, near Oxton, has an older claim and fits the early descriptions better. The earliest Life of Cuthbert says that he worked for a while as a shepherd in the hills near the River Leader.[8] The Leader flows directly below Channelkirk on the southern slopes of the Lammermuirs, and in 1242 the monks of Dryburgh built a chapel of St Cuthbert there, claiming that this was his childhood home and the oldest parish in the valley. The Berwickshire Naturalists visited Channelkirk on the same day as their outing to Brotherstone but tactfully avoided contradicting Mr Sime. Channelkirk people are more forthright. In 1992 they celebrated their 750th anniversary with a tapestry of parish life through the ages, including a prominent figure of Cuthbert in the hills opposite the church.

Like most children, Cuthbert loved games, especially wrestling, running and jumping. He was also very competitive at this stage and loved to win.[9] Later, he became ill with a badly swollen knee and was unable to walk for a long time. He was cured by a passing stranger. Cuthbert had been carried outside to enjoy a little sunshine and fresh air when the stranger rode up. He asked for hospitality, then, seeing that the boy was sick, dismounted, examined him and recommended a hot bread poultice. The knee recovered and Cuthbert felt he had been visited by an angel – on horseback.[10] We are told that Kenswith brought him up from the age of eight till the day he entered the monastery, but he must have spent time away from her as well. We hear of him among a crowd of peasants on Tyneside, surviving on meagre rations with a band of warriors, and sheltering in a bothy with his horse during a long journey. All of this before he became a monk at the age of about 17.[11]

In those days, most people were religious in some way and Cuthbert grew up believing in God to some extent. This must have been partly due to Kenswith. His experience of illness and recovery seem to have been important too. Perhaps, for the first time, he felt the limits of his own energy. Certainly, Bede tells us that by the time the stranger left, he 'knew' that the power of God was not just something which happened to other people long ago in the Bible.[12]

By the time of his visit to Tyneside, he was ready to be identified as a Christian. There was a monastery there on the south side of the river and the monks used to cut wood on the north side and ferry it across on rafts. Cuthbert was watching them one day when suddenly a gale blew up and the rafts were being swept out to sea. The monks on the south shore were horrified and sent out a boat to help. When that failed, they began to pray desperately. Meanwhile, on Cuthbert's side, a great crowd had gathered, cursing and jeering. They hated the monks for their strange way of life and their new-fangled ideas. 'They have done away with the old ways of worship,' they said, 'and now nobody knows what to do.' Cuthbert did not argue with them. Instead, he appealed to their human nature: wouldn't it be more human, he asked, to pray for the terrified monks? Taken aback, and no doubt a little embarrassed at being shamed by a teenager, the people stopped jeering and knelt down beside him, religious differences set aside.[13]

Then came his days as a shepherd, and the nights too. One night, he had a strange experience. We are told that he saw light streaming from the sky and choirs of angels coming to gather up a human soul 'as if in a globe of fire' and carry it up to heaven. Cuthbert watched in amazement and as the light faded he wished he could go with them. It could be said that he fell in love that night. Hundreds of years earlier, a Hebrew song-writer had felt the same:

One thing I ask, this alone I seek,
That I may be constant in the house of the Lord all the days
of my life
To gaze upon the beauty of the Lord
And to seek him in his temple.

Cuthbert wanted that beauty, more than anything else. It's hard to know what really happened that night. We are told that it happened 'not by a natural parting of the elements but by the sight of his spiritual eyes'. Also, that Cuthbert was in the habit of praying in the hills at night 'with pure faith and with a faithful heart'.[14] In other words, this did not come out of the blue or without preparation. But it was not something he achieved either. Bede describes it as a 'vision'. When Cuthbert heard next day that St Aidan had died, he was sure that this was the soul he had seen. He decided to take Aidan as his model and become a monk.[15] He set out for Old Melrose.

The Iona connection

Old Melrose was a young foundation in those days too. In fact, it may well have been younger than Cuthbert himself. There may have been an old British monastery in the area once[16] but old Melrose first appears in the history books as a daughter-house of St Aidan's church at Lindisfarne, part of Aidan's mission to the Anglo-Saxons in the 630s and 640s. It all started like this.

Between 616 and 633, a large number of young Anglian nobles, relatives and supporters of the late king Ethelfrid were driven out of Northumbria by Edwin, his successor. They fled north and 'lived in exile among the Irish or Picts and were there instructed in the teachings of the Irish church and received the grace of baptism'.[17] Among these exiles were Ethelfrid's sons: Oswald, Oswy and Eanfrid, and possibly other members of their family as well. We do not know exactly where the three brothers went: possibly to the West coast where there were Irish settlers or to somewhere in Pictland. Almost certainly, Oswald spent some time on Iona. He was not their first Anglo-Saxon visitor. Already in St Columba's day there were two English monks in the community, Pilu the Saxon and Genereus the baker.[18] There were still people living on the island who remembered Columba. Adomnán's Life of St Columba had yet to be written but some of the stories in it would certainly have been known. The abbot who received the exiles would have been either Fergnae or Ségéne. Both of them knew stories about Columba and Ségéne would later hand on a story about Oswald too.[19]

In 633, it became possible for the exiles to return. Eanfrid immediately assumed his father's throne and reverted to the traditional religion of his ancestors. It was the year of Cadwalla's invasion and Eanfrid was killed in the campaign. Oswald stepped into the breach and defeated Cadwalla at the battle of Heavenfield, near Hexham. Later, he told abbot Ségéne that Columba had appeared to him on the night before the battle, wearing a shining robe which flowed out behind him covering almost the whole camp.[20] It's interesting that Bede's version of the battle of Heavenfield omits all mention of St Columba. He had become a controversial figure by then, as we shall see, so perhaps Bede quietly dropped him from the story.[21]

Almost as soon as he became king, Oswald sent to 'the Irish elders' for a bishop.[22] It's generally assumed that these elders were in Iona. Certainly, the man they sent came from there. His mission got off to a shaky start. In fact, it was a complete disaster. Soon the missionary, whose name has not been recorded, was back in Iona complaining that the Northumbrians were completely ungovernable, obstinate and barbaric.[23] Maybe they threw him out. Certainly, they didn't like what he said and refused to listen to him. The Irish held a conference to decide what to do next. This is where Aidan's name crops up for the first time. Apparently, he told the outraged missionary that he had been too severe with the Northumbrians; he should have introduced the new teaching gradually as the apostles did. Aidan recognised that people can't be bullied into changing a tried and tested outlook, especially if it involves a different lifestyle. They would change when the new ways made sense to them, and that would take time and patience.

There is a moment in meetings when all eyes turn on a particular speaker and he or she realises that they have just written their own job description. This is exactly what happened to Aidan that day on Iona:

At this, the faces and eyes of all who were at the conference
were turned towards him; and they paid close attention to
all he said, and realised that here was a fit person to be
made bishop and sent to instruct the ignorant and
unbelieving, since he was particularly endowed with
discretion, the mother of virtues.[24]

They consecrated him and sent him off to Northumbria. Some
people look for political motives in missions and no doubt they are
right to do so; but Aidan seems genuinely to have believed that
Mary's Son was a better companion in life than Woden and Thor
and that the Angles would soon recognise this – as Oswald had. It
must have been difficult for everyone at first. He spoke very little
English and Oswald had to interpret for him, but he was careful to
keep a little distance from the king as well. He asked for the island
of Lindisfarne to be his headquarters and Oswald gave it to him.
Other missionaries arrived from Ireland and/or Iona and soon the
project was under way.

Aidan knew that the best people to explain the teachings of
Jesus to the Northumbrians were people who shared the same language and culture as themselves. It was all very well bringing Irish
monks down from Iona with all their knowledge and experience,
but for the young church to take root and thrive it needed to have
local leaders, people who understood the Anglian point of view
from the inside. So Aidan instructed and trained twelve Anglian
boys to be priests to their own people. Mainly, we hear about the
boys and the men, but Aidan also persuaded women to become
religious leaders. Hilda, for example (p.120), had been on the
point of leaving for a convent in France when Aidan head-hunted
her for her own people. Oswald's sister Ebba (p.75) belongs to the
same generation, as do a number of other abbesses. One of the
twelve Anglian boys was Eata, future Abbot of Old Melrose. He
was a young abbot by today's standards, not more than about
thirty years old, 'the gentlest and simplest of men'.

The young monk
Eata was away on business when Cuthbert arrived, but Boisil was
probably quite enough for him at first. After all, it was Boisil's rep-

utation for 'sublime virtue' which had led Cuthbert to choose Melrose rather than Lindisfarne.[25] Boisil was almost certainly Irish and may have been one of Aidan's colleagues from Iona. His name seems to be an Irish form of Basil, a name known on Iona through the writings of St Basil the Great whom Columba is said to have studied and admired.[26] Boisil took Cuthbert in and, when Eata got back, they made him a monk in the Iona tradition, shaving his hair from ear to ear in the Irish style. He worked, read, prayed, got up at night to meditate and was generally young and energetic about everything.[27] Soon he would find his enthusiasm tested. He would be caught up in a power struggle within the church and would discover that leaving the world behind was not as easy as he had thought. But in the meantime he became part of the community. Most, if not all, of his novitiate was served inside the monastery. We do not hear about him going outside till later; but he would have seen Boisil getting ready for his pastoral journeys. It's possible that he accompanied him sometimes.[28] Afterwards there might be teaching based on Boisil's experiences. There would also have been visitors to the abbey: people bringing news or dropping in to use the church, or to seek help or advice from the monks.

A few years later, Eata was given a gift of land by the young king, Alchfrid, to build another monastery. Oswald had died and his brother Oswy had inherited the throne. Alchfrid was Oswy's son, under-king and heir-apparent. The land was in Ripon in Yorkshire. Eata took a number of monks from Melrose with him, including Cuthbert, who was appointed guestmaster. Then trouble blew up, the beginnings of a storm which would rage for the rest of the century. In the early 660s, Alchfrid came under the influence of a young man called Wilfrid, who had lived on Lindisfarne for a while but left without becoming a monk. He travelled through Gaul, where he was hugely impressed with the lifestyle and generosity of the Archbishop of Lyons, then on to Rome where he studied before returning to Lyons. There he received the tonsure in the Roman style and became a monk. Returning to Northumbria, he went to see Alchfrid and made a great impression. The two became firm friends. Alchfrid gave Wilfrid the monastery at Ripon which he had previously given to Eata. There was just one problem: Eata was still there; but Wilfrid managed to convince Alchfrid that the style of Christianity which his father and uncle had brought from Iona was backward and inferior to the continental variety and that the monastery at Ripon should be run along continental lines.[29] So it came about that in 660 Eata, Cuthbert and the rest were 'thrown out' of Ripon and Wilfrid was appointed abbot instead.[30] If he came to Ripon before they left, Cuthbert may well have met him in his capacity as guestmaster. I wonder what he made of this highly intelligent, widely-travelled young man, the same age as himself, eager for leadership within the Church.

Eata and his monks returned to Old Melrose, but the storm was far from over. It would break a few years later at the Synod of Whitby. In the meantime, for Cuthbert, other challenges came thick and fast. Some kind of epidemic or 'plague' was ravaging the country and he caught it. He almost died but made it through the night and was awake next morning, asking for his shoes and stick. It was some time before he was able to walk without support. It was the end of his youthful vigour, but Bede thought he had gained something as well: 'his strength was made perfect in weakness' like the apostle Paul.[31] He had been ill before, but never so seriously and as layers of unimportant things fell away, along with his poise and dignity, he learned the contours of helplessness and the goodness of other people. But there was more to come.

Boisil saw that he was better and reassured him that he would never suffer from plague again. He was about to lose his mentor though. Boisil had just discovered the first symptoms of the illness in himself and urgently wanted to pass on the essence of his teaching. He suggested they read together for a while each day, from a commentary on John's Gospel, and 'perhaps discuss it if we want'. Discussion was less important to him at this stage than listening. Over the next seven days, 'they dealt not with the profound arguments but with the simple things of the faith which worketh by love'.[32] Perhaps it was through this shared reading that Boisil got an insight into Cuthbert's future. Perhaps he could see that here was a young person who had a gift for love in action, not just for 'leaving the world behind'.

It was said afterwards that Boisil had hinted that Cuthbert would be a bishop one day. It's conventional to say that saints are reluctant to be leaders, but every detail of Bede's portrait points that way. Some of his reasons seem quite negative: Cuthbert did not want to get involved with the cares of the world, and he was afraid that love of money might get the better of him. The only solution, he thought, was to live on a desert island.[33] However, desert islands can be more than just an escape, and solitude was to be more important in his life than perhaps Boisil realised. Almost at once, however, Cuthbert found himself having to go out from the monastery to take on Boisil's duties as Prior. He began to travel widely, preaching, teaching and visiting.

Sometimes he went on horseback, more often on foot. He might be away for a week, a fortnight, even a month at a time, living with the 'rough hill folk'. Bede tells us that this was a labour of love to him and that he made a point of searching out 'those steep rugged places in the hills which other preachers dreaded to visit because of their poverty and squalor'.[34] The people in the villages had had a terrible time. The plague which killed Boisil had raged through the whole countryside and people were devastated by it. When the Christian God seemed to be letting them down, many of them had gone back to the old gods in desperation. The normally mild-mannered Bede fulminates against their 'amulets and incantations' but Cuthbert tried to restore their confidence by persuasion and above all by caring for them himself. Perhaps it was because he had so recently been through a similar experience that he knew when to speak and when to keep quiet. He was probably the last person some of them wanted to see, but there was a custom of coming to hear a Christian priest whenever there was one in the area, and Cuthbert somehow managed to get through to them, by his manner and example, as much as by what he said. Bede says he had the face of an angel, and perhaps some of them really did look at him and see a messenger of God. They ended up telling him 'the closest secrets of their heart' and he spent a lot of time listening to people and hearing confessions.[35] This is one of the first signs we get that Cuthbert had been ordained. He visited well-off people as well as the poor, and not only in connection with the plague. He was a regular visitor at the home of Eadswith and Hildmer long before Eadswith became unwell (p.65) with a complaint they were both too ashamed to mention.[36]

Crisis and change: the Synod of Whitby

Meanwhile, the storm which had been brewing at Ripon had finally broken and was threatening to tear the young church apart. Wilfrid had persuaded Alchfrid that his father was keeping Easter at the wrong time. Oswy followed the monks of Lindisfarne and Iona but Wilfrid had recently learned a new way of calculating dates in Rome. It had long been known that there were different views on this. In Catterick, in the time of Aidan, a deacon from Canterbury kept the Roman Easter undisturbed. In the next generation, Aidan's successor, Finán, lost his temper with a fellow-Irishman who tried to persuade him that Iona was out of step. This man, Rónán, probably came from the south of Ireland where they had been using the new method since the 630s. Finally, Alchfrid's mother, Eanfled, had been brought up with the Roman method in Kent and continued to keep it.[37] The differences were inconvenient, but they had been tolerated. Now, however, the tensions became acute, with Alchfrid and Eanfled following one tradition, Oswy the other. More importantly, since Alchfrid was heir to the throne, the whole orientation of the Northumbrian church looked set to change. Instead of looking to Iona and Ireland for spiritual leadership, they might now be looking to the continent and Rome.

Oswy would have had to weigh the political implications as well. What would happen on his north-western frontier if he offended the Irish and the Picts? Could he afford to alienate his favourite son? Would there be benefits in closer links with the continent – or in having his spiritual authorities a little further away? It must have been a difficult decision. He had close ties with Ireland himself, including a son by a woman of the powerful Uí Néill dynasty. It was under the influence of Irish Christians that he and his brothers had abandoned their parents' gods. He had been instructed and baptised by Irish teachers and spoke Irish fluently.[38] Bede presents him as thoroughly pro-Irish and he may well have been so up to this point.

It's not clear whose idea it was to call for a synod to put an end to the dispute. It was held in Hilda's monastery at Whitby in 664, just before the plague of that year.[39] Wilfrid spoke for the Roman side, supported by Alchfrid, Eanfled and a visiting bishop, Agilbert, originally from Gaul. Colmán, Bishop of Lindisfarne, spoke for the Iona tradition. With him were Hilda and Cedd, a 'venerable' Irish-trained bishop who also acted as interpreter. Oswy sat in the middle as arbiter. The final decision would be his.

This wasn't just an argument about Easter. They also argued about what style of haircut the monks should wear: should it be the Irish ear-to-ear tonsure, or the Roman one on the crown of the head? This seems trivial to us today, but it was part of a passionate argument about authority, with both sides seeing themselves as guardians of tradition and orthodoxy. Colmán began by saying that he had learned these customs from his superiors. All his forebears had used them, he said, people beloved by God. They followed the apostle John, the disciple whom Jesus loved, who leaned upon his breast at the Last Supper. In other words, it was a tradition which went back to the first Easter, to the authority of one of Jesus's closest friends.

Wilfrid invoked St Peter and St Paul, both of whom 'lived, taught, suffered and are buried' in Rome. He went on to claim that everyone observed Easter at the same time as the Romans except 'these Irishmen and their partners in obstinacy the Picts and the Britons'. This was not quite true. Gaul was still working on a different system, closer to the Roman one but diverging from it every now and then.[40] Wilfrid may or may not have known this but he moved on, accusing the Irish of stupidity – a terrible insult to a people who had taught Latin, literacy and scripture all over Britain and Western Europe for generations.

It quickly became apparent that Colmán was no match for Wilfrid as a debater. Every time he cited an authority, Wilfrid undermined his understanding of it, till it appeared that Iona really followed no authority but their own, based on muddle and ignorance. He stopped just short of calling Columba a magician and an impostor, then patronised the 'primitive simplicity' of his followers who would surely have changed their ways if any Catholic reckoner had come to them.[41] This subtle appropriation of the word Catholic would have puzzled Colmán and set alarm bells ringing. The Irish did not think of themselves as a separate communion. Iona was being accused of heresy. Wilfrid put on a dazzling display of erudition and by the end of it Oswy had opted for St Peter and the Roman Easter. The 'cosmic horizon' was much more real to people in those days and Oswy seems to have been swayed finally by the belief that St Peter, rather than St Columba, held the keys to the afterlife. Six years later, on his death-bed, he made plans to go to Rome, if he recovered. His hope was to die there and he even asked Wilfrid to accompany him.[42] Back in 664, however, it quickly became obvious that Oswy had no intention of listening to Wilfrid – far less the Pope – on every matter relating to the Church.

The Synod of Whitby was a turning point for Christians in England but it was not the end of the 'Celtic Church', far less of Celtic Christianity. Most scholars now accept that British, Irish and Pictish Christians did not think of themselves as belonging to a separate 'Celtic Church'.[43] As for Celtic Christianity, nearly all of its most famous surviving texts had yet to be written: all of the Lives of Patrick, Brigit and Columba; most of the famous hymns including 'St Patrick's Breastplate' and 'Be Thou My Vision'; all the voyage literature including the *Voyage of St Brendan*; all the homilies, devotional poetry and biblical apocrypha; probably all of the nature poetry. Anglo-Saxon Christians did not suddenly turn their backs on their Celtic neighbours. The Ruthwell Cross, the Lindisfarne Gospels and many other fine works of art show continuing links between Anglo-Saxon and Celtic culture. Anglian students continued to study in Ireland and there were at least two Anglo-Saxon monasteries there as well.[44] By the end of the century, Adomnán, Abbot of Iona, would visit the Northumbrian court, and be welcomed by a new king, Aldfrith, alias Fland Fina, Oswy's half-Irish son who had studied in Ireland and Iona.[45]

Back in the mid-660s, however, a bishopric was vacant – Colmán's. Unable to accept the king's decision, the Irishman went back to Iona, taking a large part of the community with him.[46] A new bishop was chosen, another with Celtic connections – Tuda, who had been trained and consecrated in southern Ireland.[47] He died soon afterwards during the plague. At this point, Alchfrid chose Wilfrid to be bishop and sent him to be consecrated in Gaul. Oswy, meanwhile, selected a different candidate. Perhaps they intended the bishopric to be divided in two, perhaps they disagreed, but while Wilfrid was out of the country, Alchfrid either died or fell from favour and Oswy's candidate, Chad, was consecrated in London by one Saxon bishop and two British ones, neither of whom accepted the Roman Easter.[48] When Wilfrid came back in 666, he was outraged. He tried to claim the bishopric from Chad but, with no royal patron to support him, he failed and retired to Ripon to lick his wounds.

Twice in his life, Wilfrid would appeal to the Bishop of Rome over decisions taken against him by kings and local bishops, including the Archbishop of Canterbury. Both times he was successful, but the papal ruling was simply ignored on the ground. Wilfrid was highly successful in other areas of his life, as a missionary for example, and as a patron of the arts, but no one seems to have been able to get on with him for long and it's hard to escape the conclusion that the Synod of Whitby was at least as much a clash of personalities as a clash over the extent of papal authority.[49]

The new Prior of Lindisfarne

There is no evidence that Cuthbert was present at the synod of Whitby. It's questionable whether the prior of a small monastery like Melrose would have been invited in any case. Boisil had probably died a year or two earlier and Cuthbert would have been fully occupied, travelling and preaching. News would have filtered through of course, and we can only imagine how the Melrose community felt as they heard it: Colmán humiliated, the royal house cutting its ties with Iona, the Lindisfarne community torn apart.

It was about this time that Cuthbert mysteriously disappeared. One day, apparently, he got into a boat 'privately and secretly' and sailed away.[50] Bede covers this episode up, probably because leaving the monastery without permission did not fit with his idea of a saint. However, the Anonymous is quite open about it, if rather vague. We do not know where Cuthbert went or why he did it. Perhaps he needed time on his own, a kind of retreat, to balance the busy, sometimes harrowing, work he had been doing. The Anonymous says that he was 'fleeing worldly glory' as if his grow-

Wild Goose Publications
FREEPOST SCO4513
GLASGOW
G51 3BR

2

SCW

WILD GOOSE
Publications

Work & Worship • Prayer & Politics • Music & Drama • Justice & Peace

Thank you for buying this book. If you would like to receive our catalogue, which includes books, tapes and CDs, please fill in your name and address below and return this card to us.

Name

Address

Postcode

ing reputation as a miracle-worker was becoming a burden. That may well have been part of it, but I wonder if there was not another reason as well. It's possible that he was troubled by the outcome of the synod and needed time to reflect, away from the pressures and arguments which must have been going on in Melrose at the time. There were opportunities for able young men in the wreckage of Aidan's work, but would he take them?

Before Colmán left, he asked that Eata should take over from him as Abbot of Lindisfarne. Since Eata had been trained by Aidan, this would provide at least some continuity with the past, but he had to continue as Abbot of Melrose as well, a double responsibility.[51] Perhaps it was he who 'invited and constrained' Cuthbert to leave his bolt-hole and accept the position of Prior of Lindisfarne.[52] Cuthbert already had some experience of being a prior, so in some ways it was a job he knew well. He still went out and about, visiting people in the countryside, but now he had to deal with serious problems inside the monastery caused by the recent split. Part of his job was to teach the monks the 'true Rule' of the monastic life. It's easy to assume that this means a more romanised Rule than the one they had been using, and so it may have been in some respects. What is surprising is that it seems to have been too fierce for some of them. If Cuthbert had wanted to introduce a romanised Rule, the obvious choice would have been a version of the Rule of St Benedict which is usually thought of as less ferocious than Irish Rules of the period.[53] Cuthbert did not go for that. Instead, he got the community to write their own Rule under his direction, and it's very interesting and puzzling that some of them still found it too hard.[54]

What may have happened is that the more ascetically-minded monks went back to Ireland with Colmán, leaving some who genuinely accepted the new ways and others who simply hoped for an easy life. There were many people in monasteries and convents in those days who were not there out of choice: they might be there in fulfilment of a vow made by their parents, or because they were elderly or disabled, or simply unmarried. Cuthbert found some of them soft and lazy; nor did he like their expensive taste in clothes. It has been suggested that he came to impose a drab Roman uniformity on their glorious Celtic variety but this is not the case. It was the expense he did not like.[55] He thought that monks should dress simply in natural undyed wool. If anything, he was being a little too Celtic for them.

There were some stormy meetings. Bede puts the best complexion on them, but it's not clear that Cuthbert always handled them well. Instead of arguing, we are told he would get up and walk out 'calm and unruffled', then make exactly the same point again the following day. It must have been infuriating. He could also be a little self-righteous. When other monks complained about having their sleep disturbed, he replied that he was always pleased when that happened as it gave him the opportunity to do something useful.[56] Bede finds this admirable and perhaps it was, by monastic standards of the day, but it's easy to understand why the new prior was not always popular with everyone.

Outside of meetings and travelling about, he worked with his hands and prayed. Bede says that he relieved the 'tedium' of his vigils and recitations by walking about. Suddenly we see beyond the enthusiasm and the hero-worship to a human being, a monk who occasionally gets bored with spiritual exercises. He could be emotional at times as well. Tears came to his eyes during the liturgy, especially while he was saying mass, and he would sometimes be so moved by what people told him during confessions that he would weep and even do their penance alongside them.[57] So much for the myth of the unemotional Anglo-Saxon male. Nowadays, most people would probably be embarrassed if their priest or minister burst into tears in front of them, but Cuthbert predates the stiff upper-lip. Tears were often seen as a blessing in the medieval world, and men as well as women made far less effort to hide them.

The hermit of Inner Farne

Cuthbert had long been aware of an inner world which had at least as much reality for him as the world outside. He believed that God was present in both. The first time he thought he 'heard' the Spirit speaking to him, it was through a remark made to him by another child. After that, he began to 'hear' it 'in recesses of his heart': he 'came to know the Lord perfectly and opened the ear of his heart to receive his word'.[58] It's easy to skip over this as if it were just a pious phrase, but I think Bede is trying to describe an experience which is extremely difficult to describe and which makes many people sceptical or uneasy. Bede recognised it though, and it is very much part of the Christian tradition, especially the mystical tradition. It can be dangerous to go down this path alone. Most people need an experienced guide, as Boisil was for Cuthbert. But once he noticed this kind of 'listening', he wanted to live in such a way as to make it possible: in everyday life, in the monastery and the hermitage and also in his meetings with other people. It was an experience which shaped his life.

When he was about 42, after he had been on Lindisfarne for about twelve years, he obtained permission to do something which he had wanted to do for a long time: become a hermit. There is no doubting his ability to live in community. He had done it for years, first in Melrose, then on Lindisfarne, and he was used to mixing with all kinds of people outside the monastery as well. So why did he want to live alone? Two things might have drawn him: the desire to listen more closely to the voice of the Spirit, and the desire to follow in the footsteps of St Aidan.

It was Aidan who first used Inner Farne as a retreat.[59] This small island off Bamburgh was easily reached from Lindisfarne by boat. It's not clear how much time Aidan actually spent there, but island retreats were very much part of the Irish tradition. Sensibly, Cuthbert did not go straight to Inner Farne. Instead, he lived for a while on the fringes of the monastery – probably on the small island known nowadays as St Cuthbert's Isle. Only when he was used to that degree of solitude did he move further away. He loved it there, but if he went even partly as an escape Farne would show him his own shortcomings soon enough (p.143).

There's a delightful irony in Bede's description of Cuthbert as king of the island, building a 'city worthy of his power'. He made a circular rampart with two huts inside it – a prayer hut and a hut to live in. The rampart was built in such a way that he could only see the sky. There was a guest-hut near the landing place – and over the years he received a lot of visitors. To begin with, bread was brought out to him from Lindisfarne, but later he asked for gardening tools and began growing his own wheat.[60] When visitors arrived, he would heat water and wash their feet. Sometimes they returned the compliment – a real penance as he hardly ever took off his boots.[61]

It is said that when Augustine of Canterbury (p.125) first arrived in England, the Britons consulted a 'holy hermit' about what to do.[62] Cuthbert came to be seen in exactly the same kind of way, and people travelled long distances to talk to him:

> *They confessed their sins, confided in him about their temptations, and laid open to him the common troubles of humanity they were labouring under... Spirits that were chilled with sadness he could warm back to hope again... Those beset with worry he brought back to thoughts of the joys of heaven...* [63]

On one occasion, he left the island for a meeting with Abbess Aelfflaed (p.120) on Coquet Island, a little to the south. After a while, though, he stopped coming down to the landing stage and rarely spoke to anyone. He enjoyed seeing people through the window but eventually he blocked it up and only opened it 'to give a blessing or for some definite need'. He insisted that there was nothing specially exalted about the hermit life, though others clearly thought that there was.[64]

What are we to make of all this today? Very few people could live as Cuthbert did and survive with their mental and physical health intact. No responsible friend or spiritual director would allow it. Was he mad? Are the stories about him exaggerated? The answer to the second question is almost certainly yes. Lives of saints do tend to exaggerate. As to the first question: some of Cuthbert's behaviour might be taken today as a sign of mental illness. The loneliness must have been terrible at times. One winter, an epidemic visited the monastery and most of his friends there died.[65] It would be surprising if he did not go through layers of depression and anxiety during the nine years he spent on Inner Farne, as well as experiencing moments of elation. The Anonymous denies this: 'in all conditions he bore himself with unshaken balance'; but he cannot possibly have known what Cuthbert was like when there was no one there to see him.[66] Having said that, I think we should be wary about applying present-day standards to someone whose culture and mind-set were so very different from our own.

In general, medieval Europeans were much more pre-occupied with life after death than most of us are today, and some were willing to go extraordinary lengths to get to heaven. This had been one of Cuthbert's original reasons for entering the monastery. The hermit life might appear to be just another step along the same road. But there's another side to it. Just as there are explorers and pioneers in the everyday world, so perhaps there are explorers of the world of soul and spirit. To believers, one way to be open to these worlds is through contemplation. There are interesting similarities between Cuthbert's retreat on Farne and the retreats which are going on today on that other Holy Island off Arran in the west of Scotland. There, monks and nuns of the Tibetan Buddhist tradition spend years in meditation – arguably, the eastern equivalent of contemplation. The cells of their new retreat centre are being constructed in such a way that when they are sitting down, they, like Cuthbert, will only be able to see the sky. Buddhism and Christianity have many differences, but they share a traditional belief that solitary contemplation/meditation is not just for the benefit of the person doing it, but for the rest of the world too. The people who came to Cuthbert for help believed this, but they also believed that he was helping them even when he did not see anyone, by his prayers and by his radical self-giving. The test came in 684 when he was asked to leave the hermitage and start relating to other people 'normally' again. The fact that he managed to do this at all suggests that the hermit experience was not damaging for him, as it might have been, but creative.

Cuthbert, shepherd of souls

The Victorian artist William Bell Scott painted his impression of Cuthbert being invited to become Bishop of Lindisfarne. The setting is Inner Farne on a late summer's day, with swallows wheeling in a blue sky. In the centre, Ecfrith, Oswy's son and king since 671, looks young and earnest as he presses Cuthbert to accept the bishop's crozier he has brought with him. Cuthbert waves him away with one hand, while the other holds on to the spade he has been using to harvest his onions. He has been elected bishop in his absence and has ignored letters and messengers summoning him to appear. Now the king himself has arrived, together with

Trumwine, Bishop of the Picts, and a small deputation of other dignitaries. Finally, and in much distress, Cuthbert agrees.[67] This unwillingness may be something of a convention, but Bede was writing at a time when squabbling over bishoprics was all too common. He wants us to understand that Cuthbert did not become a religious leader out of a secret desire for power and status.

The world had moved on while he was away. The exotic figure of Theodore of Tarsus, Archbishop of Canterbury, had visited Lindisfarne and re-consecrated Finán's church in honour of St Peter.[68] Eata was now a bishop.[69] Wilfrid had been to Rome and back, had spent nine months in prison in Dunbar on Ecfrith's orders, and was now conducting a successful mission in Sussex.[70] The new monastery at Wearmouth had gone from strength to strength under a form of the Benedictine Rule. Its first abbot, Benedict Biscop, continued his regular trips to Rome, bringing back manuscripts for the library, relics and other treasures for the church. Recently, he had brought back a teacher, John the Cantor, to instruct in music and liturgy. His workshops drew interest from far and wide.[71] Across from Wearmouth, another new monastery had been built at Jarrow, and in one of these communities a twelve-year-old boy called Bede was growing up. He accepted without question the Roman Easter and the new use of the word 'Catholic' but it was not Wilfrid whom he admired most as he grew older, but the gentler abbots of his own community, and Aidan, and, above all, Cuthbert.

Cuthbert may never have heard of Bede, but news of other events would have reached the island. Indeed, his visitors may have confided more in him, as an outsider, than they did in each other. Perhaps he felt like a bit of a relic at times, with his roots in the Irish past, but he was also aware that pockets of bitterness remained over the Whitby affair.[72] He accepted the situation himself and wanted to let old wounds heal, but perhaps his training and reputation made him acceptable to both sides.

He accepted his new calling, following in the footsteps of St Aidan and remembering that Boisil had thought him fit for it. It was a tall order: he was expected to be able to protect people with his prayers, inspire them with good teaching and, above all, practice what he preached. Also, he was responsible for more people than ever before. He came to see this as a kind of prayer in itself, remembering that Jesus said there were only two basic command-ments: 'Love God' and 'Love your neighbour as yourself'.[73] He took to the road, consecrating chapels, ordaining priests, confirm-ing the recently baptised and meeting with colleagues. We hear of him back in Melrose for a meeting with Eata, and again some-where between Hexham and Carlisle for a two-day confirmation event (p.123).[74] In Carlisle, he was given a civic reception with visits to the city walls and the Roman fountain. He had an audi-ence with Queen Iurminburg (p.120) on the same occasion and was with her when news came through of her husband's death. Ecfrith had been killed by the Picts, fighting an ill-advised and brutal campaign.[75] When Iurminburg became a nun, it was Cuthbert who received her vows.

He continued to act as a soul friend or spiritual director. One of the people who came to him was a hermit called Hereberht, who used to visit him every year from his island on Derwentwater in the Lake District. Hearing that Cuthbert was in Carlisle, he took the opportunity to speak with him. At about this time, Cuthbert seems to have had a premonition of his own death or became aware of some serious health problem in himself. Realising that he might not see Hereberht again, he decided to warn him. The hermit became distraught, begging Cuthbert not to leave him, and to pray that they might die at the same moment and be reunited in heaven. We have already seen how Cuthbert could be emotional on occasions. Here we see him gently accepting an emotional out-burst from another man.[76]

Bede recounts various miracles during this period – mainly miracles of healing and prophecy – but he is particularly careful to emphasise practical goodness as well:

> He delivered 'the poor man from him that was too strong for him, the poor and the needy from him that despoiled them'. He took care to comfort the sad and faint-hearted and to bring back those that delighted in evil to a godly sorrow. He strictly maintained his old frugality and took delight in preserving the rigours of the monastery amid the pomp of the world. He fed the hungry, clothed the destitute and had all the other marks of a perfect bishop.[77]

Bede is being more than a little clerical here. There's no mention of bishops in the parable about feeding the hungry and clothing the naked. These are simply the activities of any good man or woman.[78] But Bede was unhappy with the quality of Christian leadership in his own day, and would soon write an outspoken letter on the subject to the Bishop of York. There were many small farms and villages in the hills, he said, where people did not see a bishop, or any other minister, for years on end, but still had to pay their taxes to the Church.[79] As so often, he is using Cuthbert as a model, to make a point.

Cuthbert's death

Cuthbert went back to his island to die. There was an Irish custom of 'making your soul' before death and Cuthbert may have been doing something similar.[80] At the time, his last days were seen as a kind of terrible preparation of the joys of heaven. He wanted to be alone, but one March day very near the end, a storm blew up, cutting him off completely. They found him five days later, lying in the guesthouse, still conscious and barely able to speak. Herefrith, who wrote about it afterwards, did not dare to ask him what it had been like. His Cuthbert has all the lightness and fragility of a skeleton leaf.

His 'last words', as they have come down to us, contain a harsh sentence about not associating with people who have 'wandered from the unity of the catholic faith... through not celebrating Easter at the correct time'.[81] Maybe he did say this. Living with the tension between Rome and Iona was one of his life's challenges and there was still ill-feeling about it, even in Bede's day. Some scholars think this is propagandist material inserted into the Life, and the phrase about Easter does sound more like Bede than Cuthbert. The rest of his final teaching gives the impression of a strong compassionate spirit, appealing for charity above all.

The beginnings of the pilgrimage

Cuthbert's body was taken back to Lindisfarne for burial. During his lifetime, a friend of his, an abbess called Verca, had made him a beautiful garment which he never wore but put aside for his burial. This may have been the 'priestly robe' in which his body was dressed. They also put shoes on his feet 'in readiness to meet Christ' and buried him in a stone coffin to the right of the altar in Finán's old church, now the church of St Peter.[82] The first miracle stories began soon afterwards. People believed that God had cured them through Cuthbert's posthumous prayers. It was customary in those days for the bodies of saints to be 'translated' after a few years, i.e. for their bones to be enshrined above ground in a special part of the church. When they went to do this with Cuthbert's body in 698, they found that it had not decayed at all. This was taken as a further sign of his sanctity and the body was re-wrapped, put in a new coffin covered with figures of Jesus and Mary, the apostles, evangelists and archangels, and placed on the floor of the sanctuary.[83]

Now the pilgrimage really began in earnest. There had been pilgrims to Lindisfarne before. Bede tells us that the boy strapped to the cart (p.150) was brought first of all, to be prayed for at 'the relics of the martyrs'. Now, however, the abbey had a local saint, someone known and remembered, one of the family, as it were. They commissioned an unnamed monk, the Anonymous, to collect people's memories of him and weave them into a Life. At about the same time, the Lindisfarne Gospels were created 'in honour of God and St Cuthbert'. From then till the Viking raids, a steady stream of pilgrims came to pray at his tomb. The island became known as Holy Island. When the raids forced them to move, they took his body with them and by the end of the tenth century Durham rather than Holy Island had become the centre of the St Cuthbert pilgrimage. However, Lindisfarne continued to attract visitors, as did Inner Farne.

People have often remarked on the contrast between Cuthbert's life and the opulence of the grave-goods found in his coffin when it was opened in the 19th century. How are we to account for the fine silks, the gold pectoral cross and so on? Perhaps we should doubt everything which Bede and the Anonymous ever wrote about his lack of worldly ambition and simple lifestyle. However, not all the objects found in the tomb were there from the beginning, and they may show the wealth the Lindisfarne monastery could draw on rather than the wealth of Cuthbert himself. The story of Verca's garment suggests another possible explanation. At some stage a tiny portable altar (p.123) and copy of John's Gospel were also placed next to the body. I like to think he would have been happy with these.

Notes

1   Bede, *Life*, 6.

2   D.H. Farmer (*The Age of Bede*) dates Bede's verse *Life* to 716 and his prose *Life* to 728, revising Charles Plummer's earlier dating of 721.

3   Anon. 2.7.

4   Colgrave, *Two Lives of St Cuthbert*, Cambridge, 1940, 322. The sixth-century Irish nun, St Íte, is said to have fostered several children including St Brendan 'the navigator'.

5   Bede, *Life*, 4-6. Almost certainly, the shepherding story is intended to pre-figure Cuthbert's later life as a shepherd of souls, but that need not mean it is untrue.

6   Colgrave, *Two Lives*, 324; Anon.2.7.

7   *History of the Berwickshire Naturalists' Club*, 1882–4, 10, 309–310; 1930, 27, 172.

8   Anon. 1.5.

9   Bede, *Life*, 1.

10 Bede, *Life*, 2. Anon. 1.4.

11 Bede, *Life*, 3 and 5. Anon. 1.7; According to Colgrave, this is the Tyne at Newcastle rather than the Tyne in Berwickshire. *Two Lives*, 342.

12 Bede, *Life*, 2.

13 Bede, *Life*, 3.

14 Anon. 1.5.

15 Cf. Ernéne's vision in Adamnán's *Life of St Columba*, 3.23.

16 Christopher D. Morris, 'The Early Historic Period' in Donald Omand, *The Borders Book*, Edinburgh, 1995, 60.

17 Bede, *EH* 3.1.

18 Adomnán, *Life of St Columba*, 3.22; 3.10.

19 Adomnán, op.cit. 1.1.

20 ibid.

21 Bede, *EH* 3.2.

22 Bede *EH* 3.3.

23 Bede, *EH* 3.5.

24 ibid.

25 Bede, *Life*, 6.

26 Colin Ireland, 'An Irishman hidden in the works of Bede', *Peritia* 5, 1986, 400–3; Thomas Owen Clancy and Gilbert Markus, *Iona*, Edinburgh, 1995, 106–7.

27 ibid.

28 Later, we hear of a boy travelling as part of Cuthbert's company on his pastoral journeys, but it's not clear that the boy was a monk. Anon. 2.5.

29 Eddius Stephanus, *Life of Wilfrid*, 2–8.

30 Bede, *Life*, 8.

31 Ibid; 2 Corinthians, 12.9.

32 Bede, ibid. quoting Galatians 5.6.

33 Bede, ibid.

34 Bede, *Life* 9; *EH* 4.27.

35 ibid; ibid.

36 Some people think Cuthbert visited Hildmer and Eadswith from Lindisfarne. This is possible, but both Bede and the Anonymous place it alongside stories from the Melrose area.

37 Bede, *EH*, 3.25.

38 ibid.

39 The plague of 664, as described by Bede (*EH* 3.27) leaves little time for Cuthbert to take over Boisil's duties, spend some time on retreat, and then move to Lindisfarne. Perhaps Boisil died in a different epidemic, a year or two earlier.

40 They were using Victoricus of Aquitaine's Paschal tables which had been brought from Rome in 457 but were no longer used there. Gaul persisted with them till c.742–814. *Oxford Dictionary of the Christian Church:* Paschal Controversies.

41 Bede, *EH* 3.25. Wilfrid quotes Matthew 7.21–3 but omits the phrase 'workers of iniquity'. The Irish tonsure was sometimes referred to disparagingly as 'the tonsure of Simon Magus' i.e. Simon the magician, the self-styled 'power of God' who appears in Acts 8.9–24. It is thought that Irish monks retained or adopted the traditional hairstyle of the druids, often called magi in Latin.

42 Bede, *EH* 4.5.

43 Kathleen Hughes, 'The Celtic Church: is this a valid concept?', *Cambridge Medieval Celtic Studies* I, 1981, 1–20; Wendy Davies, 'The Myth of the Celtic Church', in N. Edwards and A. Lane, *The Early Church in Wales and the West*, Oxford, 1992, 12–24; Ian Bradley, *Celtic Christianity*, Edinburgh, 1999, 90–153; Oliver Davies, *Celtic Christianity in Early Medieval Wales*, Cardiff, 1996, 1–6.

44 Bede, *EH*, 3.27; 4.4.

45 Bede, *Life* 24; *EH* 4.26; 5.15; Anon. 3.6.

46 Bede, *EH* 4.4. They eventually settled on the island of Inishbofin.

47 Bede, *EH* 3.26.

48 Bede, *EH* 3.7; 3.29.

49 For more on Wilfrid, see *St Wilfrid at Hexham*, ed. D.A. Kirby, Newcastle, 1974.

50 Anon. 3.1.

51 Bede, *EH* 3. 26.

52 He was 'invited' and 'constrained'. Anon. 3.1; Bede, *Life* 16.

53 For example, the Rule of Uinniau and the Rule of Columbanus. Uinniau was the British Abbot of Moville in present-day County Down. St Columbanus and St Columba are both said to have studied under him.

54 The Rule of St Benedict was not introduced till later. Anon. ibid; Bede, *Life* 16.

55 Bede, *Life* 16.

56 ibid.

57 ibid.

58 Bede, *Life* 1.

59 Bede, *EH* 3.16.

60 Bede, *Life* 19, 20.

61 Bede, *Life* 18.

62 Bede, *EH* 2..2.

63 Bede, *Life*, 22.

64 Bede, *Life* 18. cf. Bede's own remarks at the beginning of ch.17.

65 Bede, *Life* 27.

66 Anon. *Life* 3.7

67 Bede, *Life*, 24. Trumwine was not a Pict himself. He was Anglian bishop of the Pictish territories in Fife, around Abercorn, captured by Ecfrith in the early 670s. Eddius, *Life*, 19.

68 Bede, *EH* 3.25. This happened round about 678. Theodore came originally from the Greek church. EH 4.1.

69 Bede, *EH* 4.12.

70 Eddius, *Life of Wilfrid*, 24–41

71 Bede, Lives of the Abbots of Wearmouth and Jarrow, 4. *EH* 4.18.

72 See his 'last words' on unity. Bede, *Life* 39. These may not be an accurate expression of Cuthbert's own views. D.A Kirby, for example, sees them as propaganda.

73 Bede *EH* 4.28.

74 Anon. 4.5; Bede, *Life*, 32.

75 Bede, *Life* 27.

76 Bede, *Life* 28.

77 Bede, *Life* 26.

78 Matt.25.31–46.

79 Letter to Egbert, 7.

80 Mary Low, 'Canaire of Inis Cathaig', *The Radical Tradition* ed. Gilbert Markus, London, 1992, 22–28.

81 Bede, *Life* 37–40.

82 Bede, *Life* 37, 40; Anon., 4.13.

83 Bede, *Life* 42; Anon. 4.14.

Field Guide

In and around Melrose

In the high middle ages, Melrose Abbey was a pilgrimage centre in its own right. Sir Walter Scott claimed that it was one of the 'Four Heid Pilgrimages of Scotland' and so it may have been.[1] The second abbot, Waltheof (d.1159) was venerated as a saint and St Cuthbert's chapel, at Old Melrose nearby, would be visited by the same pilgrims (p.59). There was a regularly-used pilgrim route to the Border abbeys from Edinburgh, known in later times as the Girthgate or 'sanctuary road', parts of which can still be seen today. People who were on pilgrimage as an act of penance were supposed to be immune from attack as long as they were on this road. This must have been difficult for victims and their families, but the sanctuary road can be seen as an attempt to replace the old law of 'an eye for an eye and a tooth for a tooth' with something more merciful and more hopeful. It was based on a belief that people can change.

Melrose Abbey

Melrose was a Cistercian abbey. Its first monks came from Rievaulx in Yorkshire in 1136, but they were originally from St Bernard's monastery of Cîteaux in Burgundy. Bernard was one of the first founders of the order and it was their belief that most monasteries had become too wealthy and comfortable and that it was time to get back to the original Benedictine rule of prayer, poverty and manual work. One of the other founders, St Robert, wrote: 'We have abundance of food and clothing from tithes and church offerings and we have by cleverness or by force taken what belongs to the priests. Thus we fill ourselves with the blood of the people... '[2] In other words, before the Cistercian reform, most of the income from local parishes was ending up in the monasteries and local people were suffering as a result. By the time of the Reformation, many Scottish abbeys were being accused of the same thing, but in their early years they too were part of a great reform movement. Bernard and Robert embraced austerity with a will. The early diet in Cîteaux is said to have consisted of barley bread and boiled beech leaves. Gradually, they became more practical but they still tried to be prayerful and self-sufficient. They spent a large part of each day reciting the Psalms, made their own clothes from undyed

wool, ate a vegetarian diet and built simple churches of unorna-
mented stone. Somehow, they caught the mood of the moment
and soon there were hundreds of Cistercian houses all over
Europe.

The person who brought them to Scotland was King David I.
He gave the Cistercians of Melrose generous grants of land and
soon they had agricultural interests all over the Borders and
beyond. It was hard to keep to their original ideals as other gifts
flowed in from wealthy patrons, but the *Life of St Waltheof*, written
around 1207, describes the monks using their farms not just for
their own benefit but to help local people as well. Once during a
famine, we are told, huge numbers of starving men, women and
children converged on the abbey from the countryside round
about, till the fields and woods for a two-mile radius were dotted
with tents and huts, the medieval equivalent of a 'tent city' or feeding station. Waltheof provided meat and cheese for them from the
abbey's farms and opened the last reserves of the monks' own
grain to provide bread: rye from their grange at Gattonside and
corn from Eildon.[3] He is presented as a practical, compassionate
person: Job's words 'Mercy grew up with me' described him perfectly, we are told. As an old man, quite frail and leaning on a stick,
he would visit the infirmary every day and speak to all the patients
– monks, visitors and destitute poor people who had been taken in
– to make sure that everything possible was being done for them.

Monks from Melrose had a major influence in the growth of
the church in Scotland, providing abbots and bishops for communities all over the country and further afield as well. One went to
County Down in Northern Ireland, another to Orkney. In the
twelfth century, Jocelyn, Bishop of Glasgow, was a monk of Melrose. It was he who wrote the *Life of St Waltheof* and the *Life of St
Kentigern* about the city's patron saint. In those days, monks were
also sometimes used as diplomats. In 1265, King Alexander III sent
a monk of Melrose to buy the Isle of Man from the Norwegians.
His mission was successful.[4] The monks kept a record of their
activities in the *Chronicle of Melrose* which also shows an astonishing awareness of international events. They knew what was
happening in Toulouse, Rome, Venice, Sicily and Jerusalem as well
as in London and Dublin. Some of them went regularly to Cîteaux

for meetings. It was a vigorous outward-looking community.

Within a few generations, however, it had begun to drift away from its original ideals of poverty and simplicity. As early as 1180, the Chronicle reports that there was a 'great dispute' between the monks and one of their neighbours over pasture and forest rights between the Gala Water and the Leader. Four years later, it was the 'men of Wedale' by Stow who incurred their wrath over grazing rights.[5] By the 13th century some of them seem to have taken up the leisure activities of the landed gentry. They had to be told, for example, that hunting was not a suitable activity for a monk. The warning was repeated later in more detail: no hunting or bringing others to hunt; no raiding or destroying the nests of hawks or falcons.[6] Wolf-trapping was allowed to continue however, probably because of the abbey's sheep-farming interests (p.124). No doubt these rules had more to do with protecting other people's hunting rights than with modern ideas of conservation and animal welfare, but blood sports were not exactly part of the Cistercian ideal.

Abuses grew worse as the centuries wore on, but life was still austere for the monks in the 13th century. When the abbot, Father Matthew, was deposed in 1261 by the general chapter in Cîteaux, the chronicler was distressed. He does not explain exactly what had gone wrong. He says simply that Matthew had been the means of procuring property and comforts for the monks, but the comforts were meagre by today's standards: 'through him we have pittance-loaves upon the Fridays during Lent, when we fast on bread and water.' In other words, he got them a small extra ration of bread to ease the severity of their fast.

The abbey suffered badly during the later centuries of Border warfare. It was destroyed in 1385, rebuilt using some of the best craftworkers available, then badly damaged again in 1544, probably before it was finished. With the coming of the Reformation, the monastic system collapsed in Scotland and the community gradually died out. However, some of the low walls you can see today mark the foundations of the first Cistercian abbey: the outline of the cloister, the lay brothers' quarters, the kitchen, dayroom, latrine, refectory and the chapter house where the community met each morning.

The heart of Robert the Bruce

It was in the area of the chapter house in 1996 that a lead casket, said to contain a heart, was discovered during an archaeological dig. This was the famous 'heart of Robert the Bruce'. Bruce led Scotland's War of Independence in the early 14th century although, in fact, Scotland had been independent till 1296. It was then annexed by Edward I of England (p.90) and Bruce's achievement was to re-establish it as a separate country. It is said that when he was dying, he called for his friend Sir James Douglas and asked him to take his heart to the Church of the Holy Sepulchre in Jerusalem for burial. He told him that he had vowed to go on a pilgrimage to the Holy Land once the wars with England were over, but had never been able to keep his promise.[7] Douglas agreed to go on pilgrimage for him, carrying the heart. On the way he became involved in fighting the Moors in Spain and was killed. He flung the casket containing Bruce's heart into the enemy lines where it was later recovered and sent back to Scotland.

In those days, crusading was seen almost as a form of pilgrimage. Crusaders believed that by undertaking such a long and dangerous journey and by risking their lives against the 'infidel' they could be let off any penalty owing for all their past sins. It was seen as a form of penance, military style, and was supported and encouraged by the Church, not least by St Bernard himself.[8] Bruce had lived a life of violence as well as glory and had been excommunicated by the Pope. Perhaps pilgrimage appeared to him as a way of wiping the slate clean.

Towards Galashiels, on the Darnick road, is High Cross Avenue. This is said to be named after a great high cross where pilgrims, travelling from the west, got their first glimpse of the abbey. There would probably have been another high cross outside the abbey itself and by 1422 there was a cross outside the south gate of the abbey where there was already the beginning of a market square. This gate, with a gatehouse and chapel next to it, was more or less on the site of the narrow entry between Abbey Street and Melrose Square. The cross was somewhere in the square itself. Certainly, by the 16th century, a Mercat Cross existed there, surrounded on market days by street traders, flocks of sheep and cattle.[9] You can still see the base of it today, sporting a unicorn on a pole. There was another monument called 'The Haly Sing of St Waltheof' south of town, on the site of the present golf course; and an 'ancient fair' was held near there at Lammastide, the beginning of August. By 1547 this was known, for some reason, as the Scarce Thursday Fair.[10] Obscure names do tend to suggest early origins but, in the nineteenth century, local historian Alexander Jeffrey wrote that 'in the time of Popery' a fair was held in Melrose on 'Schier Thursday' and that this was Maundy Thursday, the Thursday before Easter.[11] There was another fair at Lammastide, he said. Whatever the truth of this, the Thursday of Holy Week would have been busier than usual for the little settlement at the abbey gates. It was then that poor people gathered to receive gifts of food and clothing from the monks.

Melrose Abbey. Changes planned, but at the time of writing: Parking unreserved and can get very busy Easter–October. Step from car park to pavement. 100 yds to ticket office or 40 yds to gate. Basic access difficult. Ticket office opens onto flight of 8 steps down. 'Accessible' entrance via gate nearer the car park, but have to request this at ticket office. Gate gives immediately onto soft grass, then steep slopes and uneven ground to reach the nearest hard surface. Impossible for wheelchair-users on their own and needs strong assistant. Most circulation areas grass. Several sets of 3–5 steps, but can be avoided if you're willing to settle for a shorter tour. Ramps available but not permanently in position. Paved area by site of old west door. From there to inside of church: paving, cobbles, grass, large loose gravel. Inside: concrete, paving, gravel. Benches in cloister area (may be seasonal). Good visibility once inside. Cloister area is a pleasant place to sit. To enjoy a good view of the abbey (arguably the best) without the hassle, take path called Prior's Walk alongside National Trust shop. Level, tarmac. Public park after 100 yds with bench and play area. To visit the abbey museum, ask at ticket office. Exhibits on ground and first floors. No lift. For toilets, ask at ticket office or use fully accessible one in Abbey Wynd, 80 yds from car park, open 24 hrs. Costs 20p. Radar key from attendant or bring your own if visiting out of hours.

Old Melrose

Old Melrose is not on St Cuthbert's Way itself, unfortunately, since this is where St Cuthbert became a monk. The best place to see it from is Scott's View near Bemersyde. Public transport only takes you part of the way there, so unless you have a car or a bike you should allow at least half a day extra for the round trip. You could do it as a detour off St Cuthbert's Way, between Newtown St Boswells and St Boswells. This would take you over the chain bridge at Dryburgh, left up the hill via the Wallace statue and on to Bemersyde and Scott's View, returning the same way – a round trip of nearly six miles. This is definitely the prettier route but it adds considerably to that part of the journey. The alternative is to do it as a half-day outing from Melrose before you begin. The Kelso bus is the one to catch. It runs three or four times a day from Melrose Square. Ask the driver to let you off at Clintmains. From there it's a six-mile round trip, returning either the same way or via the chain bridge at Dryburgh and the bus back to Melrose from Newtown. There are no refreshments en route apart from a fine but expensive country-house hotel and this involves another detour if you are travelling via Clintmains. If you can't face the walk, a quick hunt round the postcard shops of Melrose should produce at least one good picture of Scott's View with Old Melrose in the foreground – and there is another on the front cover of this book!

The original monastery at Old Melrose has long since disappeared. Even in its heyday, there would have been little to see, just a few whitewashed huts and a church, probably thatched and made of wood. Founded from Lindisfarne within a generation of Aidan's arrival, this was a monastery in the Celtic tradition. The name is Celtic, either British or Irish, and is thought to mean something like 'bare promontory'. There have always been some trees here, however. Fragments of ancient woodland cling to the steep banks on either side of the river.

Looking out from Scott's View today, the most obvious feature is the wavy crown of the Eildons, soft green, purple or blue depending on the time of year. Further up the valley is present-day Melrose, with the white houses of Langlee, on the outskirts of Galashiels, in the distance. In the foreground, the river loops

round the bottom of a steep cliff. There is no safe route to the
bottom and the ground shelves away quickly. A few years ago a
couple of unwary visitors had to be lifted out by helicopter after
falling through the trees, so please be very careful. Old Melrose is
the area enclosed by the loop on the far side of the river. This is
where the monastery once was. A little way downstream is the
'holy well pool' known mainly to anglers but named after a holy
well which once rose in the grounds of the abbey. At certain times
of year you will still see boats there and people casting for salmon.
More often they wear waders and fish standing in the river. A
Brother called Drythelm used to stand in much the same place, up
to his waist in water, chanting the Psalms. Austerities like this were
not uncommon in the Celtic and Anglo-Celtic traditions. Similar
stories are told of Patrick and Cuthbert, for example. Drythelm
would be out there in all weathers, even in winter, with the ice-
floes swirling around him. If anyone remarked on how cold it was
he's said to have remarked, 'I've known it colder.'[12]

Drythelm's vision

Bede tells us that Drythelm was an ordinary family man till one
day he suddenly took ill and fell into a coma. While he was in this
state he had a strange experience in which it seemed to him that
his soul went on a journey to the edge of heaven. There, his guide
told him to turn back. He returned to his body, much to the
relief of his wife and children but soon afterwards, like a Hindu
sannyasin, he left everything behind and entered the monastery at
Old Melrose. He was determined to go back to the place of light
and singing which he had glimpsed in his unconscious state. He
had 'seen' other places as well. His guide took him through the
dark valley of purgatory, past the pit of hell and into a flowery
meadow where groups of happy people were sitting around on
the grass. These, he was told, were the souls of people whose lives
had been basically good, not perfect, but good enough so that
they would join the saints in heaven at the end of time. Drythelm's
vision is similar to Dante's but much older.[13] Stories of Otherworld
visions, voyages and journeys are recorded in Britain and Ireland
from about the eighth century onwards and Drythelm's vision is
one of the earliest. Early Irish writers sometimes mention an

Otherworld region called *Mag Mell* – The Delightful Plain. Maybe Drythelm was influenced by a similar tradition and 'saw' the threshold of heaven as being like one of the old native paradises.

The monastery at Old Melrose was secluded but not cut off. The cliff below Scott's View gave it an element of protection from unfriendly visitors and north-east winds. The river enclosed it on three sides and the fourth side was marked off with an earthen rampart, but the monks had no intention of imprisoning them-selves behind it. On the contrary, they saw it as part of their job to serve the local population. St Cuthbert was only one of those who went out and about from here, teaching, healing and cele-brating the sacraments. The monastery church was open to out-siders and visitors came from quite far afield to speak to the abbot or one of the other residents. With the river on their doorstep and Dere Street less than a mile away, they were well placed for receiv-ing guests. At the end of the seventh century, Aldfrith, the half-Irish king of Northumbria, was a frequent visitor. He came mainly to listen to Drythelm.[14]

Inside the monastery there would have been a regular pat-tern of prayer and physical work: fetching water and wood, cook-ing, farming and fishing. Bede tells us that the young Cuthbert 'watched, prayed, worked and read' with the rest of the novices, so some kind of spiritual formation was provided and there were certainly books, possibly a library of some kind.[15] Bede mentions a commentary on John's Gospel which Cuthbert and Boisil read together during the plague (see p.180). There may also have been an early copy of Adamnán's *Life of St Columba*.[16] Book binding may have been one of the skills practised in the monastery work-shops. The original cover for the Lindisfarne Gospels was made by a man who lived and worked at Old Melrose: he 'impressed it on the outside and covered it as well he knew how to do'.[17] This book-binder was Ethelwald, Abbot of Melrose in Drythelm's day. He probably made the binding on Lindisfarne before taking up the abbacy, but he must surely have brought his skill with him.[18] Two former monks of Old Melrose helped Bede with stories about Cuthbert when he was writing his Life: Herefrith, who was with Cuthbert when he died, wrote an account of that. He also passed on the story of Boisil and Cuthbert studying scripture together during the plague. Sigfrith, by then an old man living in Jarrow, was with Boisil at the monastery gates when Cuthbert first arrived there to become a monk.[19]

In Cuthbert's time, the abbot was Eata, one of the twelve Anglo-Saxon boys taught by Aidan when he first came to Lindisfarne from Iona.[20] Old Melrose was, to some extent, a monastery in the Iona tradition. Changes would probably have been made to suit local conditions, and local leaders like Aidan, Boisil and Eata deserve most of the credit for its success, but it can still be seen as one of the furthest-flung parts of the Columban familia, the group of monasteries which looked to St Columba as their founder and patron saint.

In 839, Old Melrose was raided by the Pictish king, Kenneth mac Alpin, who burned down the seventh-century buildings and left a smoking ruin. It's said that in 875 or shortly afterwards, when the Lindisfarne monks were travelling with Cuthbert's body for fear of the Vikings (p.138) this was one of the places where they took refuge for a while. There's no historical evidence for this, or for Sir Walter Scott's story that they later floated him down the Tweed in a stone coffin, but the tradition remains.[21] By 1050, Old Melrose was 'desolate' once again but some buildings must still have been habitable because in 1075 Turgot, St Margaret's confessor, stayed there briefly. He was a monk of Durham cathedral and so probably had a special interest in St Cuthbert, but he was unimpressed by the place.[22] It was the Cistercians of the new Melrose Abbey who built an outlying chapel there and dedicated it to St Cuthbert, in the 13th century.

Notes

1   D. McKay, 'The Four Heid Pilgrimages of Scotland', *Innes Review* 19, 1968, 76–7.

2   *Ordericus Vitalis Historia Ecclesiastica* VIII, 25 in *Exordium*, isles edition, unit 2.

3   Jocelyn's *Life of St Waltheof* 5–6, from Walter Bower's *Scotichronicon*, written originally in the 1440s, edited in a selected version as *A History Book for Scots*, D.E.R. Watt, Edinburgh, 1998, 69–70. In Jocelyn's story, the grain is miraculously multiplied in a very obvious parallel between Waltheof and Jesus in the biblical miracle of the feeding of the four thousand.

4   *Chronicle of Melrose*, 1265–6.

5   Wedale is the old name for the village of Stow, some 7 miles north of Galashiels.

6   *Liber Sancte Marie de Melros*, Bannatyne Club, Edinburgh, 1837, I.179; Morton,

Monastic Annals of Teviotdale, 274; Alexander Jeffrey, *History of Roxburghshire*, IV.17.

7   From the English chronicler John le Bel, quoted by A. MacQuarrie along with other traditions re Bruce's heart in 'The Ideal of Holy War in Scotland 1296–1330', *Innes Review* 32.2, 1981, 83–91.

8   Pierre André Sigal, *Les Marcheurs de Dieu*, Paris, 1974, 9–10.

9   E. Patricia Dennison and Russel Coleman, *Historic Melrose*, Edinburgh, 1998, 32, 36.

10 ibid. Alternative names were Keir or Scare Thursday.

11 *An Historical and Descriptive Account of Roxburghshire*, Edinburgh, 1836, 237–242

12 Bede, *EH* 5.12.

13 Dante's *Divine Comedy* was completed at the beginning of the 14th century. He also sees a flowery meadow (*Purgatorio* 28) but it is part of Purgatory, not a region in itself.

14 Bede says that he came mainly to listen to Drythelm. ibid.

15 ibid.

16 Alan Thacker, 'Lindisfarne and the origins of the cult of St Cuthbert', 112, in *St Cuthbert: His Cult and His Community* (*CCC*), ed. Gerald Bonner, David Rollason and Clare Stancliffe, Woodbridge, 1989.

17 Aldred the priest wrote this on the last page of the Gospels when he finished translating them into Anglo-Saxon some 250 years later. Janet Backhouse, *The Lindisfarne Gospels*, 7. There is an alternative view that Ethelwald only commissioned the work. Colgrave, *Two Lives*, Cambridge, 1940, 332.

18 Backhouse, op. cit. 14

19 Bede, *Life*, 1,8, 37, 4.

20 Bede, *EH* 4.27; Bede, *EH* 3.26

21 Scott, *Marmion*, 2.14. Scott collected and elaborated on local folk traditions so he may not have invented the whole story himself. By all other accounts, however, Cuthbert's portable coffin was made of wood.

22 As Prior of Durham, Turgot was later present when Cuthbert's coffin was opened in 1104, the year of its translation to its present place behind the high altar in Durham cathedral. J. Stranks, *This Sumptuous Church*, revised ed., London, 1993, 8–10. It was Turgot who wrote the *Life of St Margaret*, the only contemporary source for her life.

Melrose to St Boswells

Trimontium

The village of Newstead, just east of Melrose, can be seen clearly from the shoulder of the Eildons. There was once a Roman camp near there known as Trimontium, or 'three hills place', after the Eildons themselves. During the second century, a centurion called Domitianus set up a series of altars here: 'To Jupiter, best and greatest... in payment of a vow', 'To Diana the queen' and 'To the god Silvanus'. It comes as no surprise that he wanted to be on good terms with Jupiter, chief of the Roman gods, but the altars to Diana and Silvanus may reflect a nervousness about the wild un-familiar country in which he found himself. Both were associated with woods and wild places, and Diana with wild animals and hunting. He asked her 'for prosperous results' and Silvanus 'for his own safety and that of his household'.[1]

At about the same time, Marcus, a cavalry officer from Vaucluse in the south of France, dedicated an altar to the Campestres, a group of three motherly-looking figures often depicted holding food in their laps.[2] Perhaps he missed his mother's Provençal cooking but he probably had an eye to the local situation as well. Triple goddesses were revered throughout the Celtic world and it's interesting that he paid his respects to them here at the foot of the Eildons. Their triple peaks may well have seemed significant to local people and incomers alike and it's possible that they were once a focus of faith and worship like the Paps of Ana or Anu in Kerry.[3]

There's no historical record of what local people believed at this time, but we know from studies of Celtic primal religion else-where that while some gods and goddesses were worshipped over a wide area, others were much more local and were associated with natural features like hills, trees, wells and rivers. There was a widespread custom of making offerings at these places. Openings in the earth were often thought of as entrances to the Otherworld and this may be why, in many Celtic areas, offerings have been found at the bottom of pits and wells.[4] This is exactly what we find in Newstead, on an astonishing scale. Nearly two hundred shafts, most of them originally wells, have been excavated so far. Some were full of rubbish but others contained what seem to be votive offerings: coins, bowls, hazel nuts, weapons, antlers and skulls of horses and other animals. We also find what looks like the debris of an uprising: human skulls, finely-wrought helmets, a Roman altar dedicated to Apollo.[5] Some of these can now be seen in the new Museum of Scotland in Edinburgh. There were peaceful offerings as well: during one recent dig, the local historian Walter Elliot opened a handful of clay from one of these pits and found himself staring at a bunch of tiny pink flowers.[6]

Dingleton Hospital

One of the most moving stories in Bede's *Life of Cuthbert* is about a woman with a mental illness. Her name was Eadswith and she was a woman of some standing, married to a local official called Hildmer.[7] She became seriously ill but did not want anyone to know about it. In those days, mental illnesses were believed to be caused by demons. This old 'explanation' reflects the fear people felt in the face of symptoms they could not understand or control. It also made people ashamed, for how, they asked, could a good person become 'possessed by demons'? Hildmer was in despair. He went to Cuthbert and asked him to send a priest to give her the last rites. Cuthbert offered to come himself and Hildmer burst into tears, beside himself with distress, but afraid that Cuthbert would think badly of the woman he loved.

It is estimated that one in four people in Britain suffer from a mental illness at some time in their lives and hesitate to tell anyone about it. One place where people worked hard to overcome the stigma and the isolation of mental illness was Dingleton Hospital on the north side of the Eildons, opposite the golf course. Dingleton began life as an ordinary Victorian asylum. Melrose people over a certain age still remember the shiver they felt walking past the locked iron gates and wondering what went on behind the high walls.

They might have been surprised at the ordinary things which people managed to do. Before the National Health Service was introduced in 1947, patients had to work for their keep: painting and decorating, cooking, working in the laundry or the hospital farm. Then, in 1949, the medical superintendent, Dr George Bell, did something which was quite unheard of. He unlocked all the doors and Dingleton became the first open mental hospital in the English-speaking world.[8] People who were well enough were encouraged to go out and join in the normal life of the town.

Under the next superintendent, Maxwell Jones, Dingleton gained an international reputation as a 'therapeutic community'. It was believed that everyone had a contribution to make, not just health professionals, but also domestics, catering staff, clerical workers and, above all, the patients. Max Jones spent a lot of time breaking down fears and prejudices. Outsiders were encouraged to visit and school-leavers began working on the wards as activity assistants.

By 1968, more people were being treated at home and community teams were developed to support them and their families. This was not community care 'on the cheap'. Two workers visited every family regularly in their own homes – an outrageous extravagance by traditional standards. But the tide was turning against big mental hospitals and by the time you read this Dingleton will have closed. People can still get help at home or in smaller units nearby; but it remains to be seen whether friends and neighbours, taxpayers and governments really will care enough to provide asylum, in the best sense, for all who need it.

Eildon Hill North

The Eildons may have been a sacred site in the late bronze age, long before the Romans arrived. Bronze axe-heads, found near springs on the west side of the hill, are thought to have been votive offerings.[9] Eildon Hill North may once have been used for seasonal festivals. This would explain the hundreds of circular huts which were built up there but never permanently occupied. Unless they were storehouses or implausibly clean workshops, it looks as though large numbers of people once wanted to be on the hill, all at the same time, but only briefly.[10] The 'Roman signal station', marked on some maps, may have had earlier uses as a ritual site. Eildon Hill North used to be described as a fort. You can still see its earthen ramparts, circling the hill like a rumpled collar. They are

over a mile long and difficult to defend so their purpose as the
ramparts of a fort has been questioned. The middle Eildon would
have made a far better one, being higher and steeper. Eildon Hill
North is now thought to have been a different kind of enclosure
with a rampart which was more symbolic than defensive, marking
the limit of a sanctuary. In other words, Eildon Hill North may
once have been a sacred place. Thousands of years later, stone
from the Eildons would be used in the building of Melrose Abbey.

The fairy world under the hill

According to one of the Border ballads, there is a fairy world
under the Eildons. The Earlston poet Thomas the Rhymer is said
to have spent seven years there, after being carried off by the fairy
queen. He re-emerges with the troublesome gift of truth so that
ever afterwards he is unable to tell a lie. The ballad begins with
the famous line:

> *True Thomas lay on Huntlie bank*
> *A ferlie he spied wi' his ee,*   (strange sight/marvel)
> *And there he saw a lady bright*
> *Come riding down by the Eildon Tree*

Her dress is of grass-green silk and she wears a velvet cloak. Tiny
silver bells jingle in her horse's mane. He thinks she is the most
beautiful woman he has ever seen. He kisses her and, with that, is
bound to her service for seven years. They ride off together till
they come to a place where the road divides in three. She tells
him, in Scots naturally, that the narrow road is the path of righteousness, beset by thorns, and few ask after it. The broad road is
the path of wickedness, though some call it the way to heaven.

> *And see not ye that bonny road*
> *That winds about the fernie brae?*   (covered with ferns)
> *That is the road to fair Elfland*
> *Where thou and I this night maun gae.*   (must go)

They ride through rivers, through the 'mirk mirk night' where there
is neither sun nor moon, just the roaring of the sea. They wade

through crimson streams 'for a' the blude that's shed on earth rins thro springs o that countrie'. It's a difficult and frightening journey, but at last they come to a fertile garden where she gives him an apple from one of the trees. 'Take this for your wages', she says, 'it will give you a tongue which can never lie.' Thomas is appalled:

> *My tongue is mine ain,' True Thomas said*   (my own)
> *A gudely gift ye wad give to me!*
> *I neither dought to buy nor sell*   (do not dare)
> *At fair or tryst where I may be.*

In other words, he won't be able do business any more. He will not find it easy to speak to princes or friends or pretty women. But the gift is given and he cannot refuse. When he comes back to earth seven years later, he speaks the truth about everything, past, present and future.

This is an 18th-century ballad about a 13th-century man, but some of the ideas in it are much older. The idea of the Otherworld under the hill is very common in early Celtic literature, as is the figure of the poet-prophet. Otherworld journeys are also a common Celtic theme, though the nearest local parallel, Drythelm's vision (p.60) is one the earliest of its kind and comes from the Anglo-Saxon tradition.[11] The story of True Thomas used to be enacted at the Melrose Festival every year till it was declared 'unhistorical' and dropped from the programme. King David I is still represented, but not the poet and the fairy woman. Their story is unhistorical of course, but the creators of the tradition knew that outward, visible events are only part of what shapes community. Passions, values and beliefs are also powerful and the world 'under the hill' can be seen as an image for all of these – for what goes on beneath the surface of our lives.

'The devil's spadeful.'

The third Eildon is mostly hidden from the Melrose side. As you go down towards Bowden, however, it stretches away to your right, a gentle expanse of heather known locally as 'the devil's spadeful'. According to legend, a wizard called Michael Scot had a demon servant who had to be kept busy. He set him a number of impossible tasks, one of which was to cleave the Eildons in three. Up to that point, we are told, there had only been one Eildon, a cone-shaped hill like the Black Hill above Earlston or Rubers Law near Hawick. The demon worked all night, scooping earth from the centre of the cone and dumping it off to one side. By morning there were three hills where there had once been one. Michael Scot was 'fair ta'en on wi' hissel' (more than a bit self-satisfied) for having ordered this minor adjustment to the landscape. His house-guests were impressed too, except for a wandering friar who asked him who created the mountains in the first place.[12] Michael Scot the wizard is based, at least partly, on a real person, Michael Scotus, who died around 1236. He was a scholar, a mathematician and an early scientist. His work disturbed people at the time and when Dante wrote his *Divine Comedy* less than a hundred years later, he placed Michael Scotus in the eighth circle of hell, among fortune-tellers and magicians.[13]

Michael Scot

Michael Scotus, known nowadays as Michael Scot, was born in Scotland, possibly in the Borders, studied abroad and, as a brilliant young graduate, became tutor to Frederick II, the young king of Sicily and future emperor. By 1217, he was in his prime, working in Toledo on a Church-based translation project. Ancient scholars like Aristotle had been virtually unknown to Christians in the West before the 12th century. Valuable treatises on medicine, maths and astronomy were simply not available in Latin or even in Greek, but they were available in Arabic. Muslim scholars had been translating them for over three hundred years.[14] As a result, Muslims had a lot of scientific knowledge which Christians looked upon with a mixture of alarm and envy: envy because much of it was exciting and useful; alarm because it challenged the idea that the Church had a monopoly on truth. The Bishops of Toledo commissioned their own translations so that they could judge the new ideas for themselves, but it was a controversial field.

The usual method in Toledo was for someone who could read Arabic to explain the text in the local language to a Latin scholar who would then compose a rough translation in Latin.[15] Many of these Arabic scholars were Jews and Michael Scotus worked with at least two Jewish translators, often referred to rather demeaningly as his 'assistants' – Abu Dawd 'the levite' and a man known simply as Andrew who helped him to translate Aristotle's great treatise on animals.[16] This was packed with new ideas about human and animal biology and was to become their most influential book. St Albert the Great, growing up in Germany at the time, would read it and go on to become the greatest Christian naturalist of the Middle Ages, but even he had to struggle against accusations of heresy.

The *Chronicle of Melrose* quotes from Michael and Andrew's translation, so there must have been a copy of it to hand.[17] There's a tradition that Michael came home to Scotland with his manuscripts and is buried in Melrose Abbey, but this is far from certain. After Toledo, he sought a conventional career in the Church and was offered the bishopric of Cashel in southern Ireland. He turned it down on the grounds that he did not speak Irish. He seems to have ended up back at the imperial court in Sicily, dreaming up strange inventions and becoming increasingly eccentric. Stories began to circulate about his 'magical powers'.

Astrology and astronomy were indistinguishable in those days; chemistry and alchemy were the same; medicine involved all kinds of strange measurements and potions. Michael Scotus was interested in all of these at a time when any kind of science was still suspect. He also worked with people of other faiths, using books written in strange characters. No wonder he acquired a reputation as a wizard. But perhaps he was a kind of pilgrim, sometimes lost, sometimes bravely on the right track, in the borderlands between the known and the unknown.

Bowden

Bowden is a quiet little village today with rows of neat white cottages round a village green. In the 18th century, it would have been much noisier. Many of the cottages were the homes of handloom weavers and the clacking of looms would have been constant from dawn to dusk. They wove locally-grown flax and bleached the linen on the green.[18] Handloom weaving went into decline with the advent of mechanisation and gradually the character of the village began to change. Some Bowden families probably

found work in the big new woollen mills which were then spring-
ing up in Selkirk, Galashiels and Hawick but it was a difficult time
for these proud hard-working people who had put shirts on the
backs of lawyers and ministers and petticoats under ladies' dresses.

At the end of the 19th century, a small group of Nigerian children came to live at Eastbank House on the St Boswells Road.
Mary Slessor the missionary was home on leave and had brought
her adopted children with her.[19] It must have been an unusual
experience for all concerned. African faces were rare in Scotland
at the time, but Mary Slessor was an unusual woman. This one-
time mill-worker from the jute mills of Dundee had become, in
effect, a reforming chief of Okoyong, on the Calabar river.[20] Her
children were either orphans or twins who would otherwise have
been abandoned at birth. There is a picture of them in the booklet on Bowden Kirk, available from Bowden Post Office, and also
on the current issue of the £10 note from the Clydesdale Bank.

Bowden was part of the lands granted to the monks of
Selkirk by the future king David I around 1119. Selkirk was the first
of the great Border abbeys, but the community did not stay there
long. After a few years they moved to Kelso, built a new abbey
and Bowden was administered from there till the Reformation. The
abbey probably provided a priest for the church and the people
paid rent, mostly in kind. In the time of Robert the Bruce, better-
off tenants gave four days' work at harvest time and another in
winter. Ploughing, harrowing and sheep-shearing were also
required and, from time to time, a cart to transport corn or wool
or to fetch peat for the abbey from Gordon Moss. Cottagers had to
sell the abbey a chicken each at Christmas and the tenants of the
four brewhouses each provided 2–3 gallons of ale.[21]

Bowden church

Bowden church is a little way south of the village, down the steep
hill which is part of St Cuthbert's Way. The visit requires a short
detour (a few hundred yards beyond the place where the footpath
turns left) but it's worth it. Places as quiet as this are rare these
days. There's a cool light and a delicately-coloured window opposite the door depicting Mary, Joseph and the three wise men, with
a shaft of light falling on the Christ-child. The text is from the song

of Zechariah: 'The dayspring from on high has visited us.'[22] There has been a church on this site for at least 850 years. Parts of the present building date from the 15th century but it has been altered and restored many times. The wooden structure against the north wall is the Laird's Loft. It provided special accommodation for the Ker family, who were lairds of Bowden after the Reformation. A dire warning is painted underneath, though for whose benefit is unclear. William Ker of Cessford (p.97) was an ancestor of this same family.

It was in Bowden church in 1888 that Scotland's first deaconess, Lady Grisell Baillie was 'solemnly set apart'.[23] She had, in fact, been doing the work of a deaconess for most of her life but the Church of Scotland had recently voted to restore the order of deaconesses which existed in the early Church and Grisell was the first to be appointed. She was 66 years old and had been teaching in Bowden Sunday School for over 20 years but she was involved in an astonishing number of other projects as well.

Bowden church. Limited unreserved parking at gate; wide level tarmac path to church door, approx. 60 yds; two very shallow steps into church; pews.

Lady Grisell Baillie

Grisell was born in 1822, the youngest of eleven children. Her father, the laird of Mellerstain, died when she was only 19, leaving her with limited prospects and a widowed mother to look after. Her brother Robert resigned his brief career in the army and came to live with them, but it was not till old Mrs Baillie died in 1865 that Grisell really came into her own. From then on, as her sister said, 'she never lay down on a sofa'.[24] While other Victorian ladies were sniffing *sal volatile* and tightening their stays, Grisell was arranging to have a bridge built or planning improvements to the water supply for Newtown St Boswells. Newtown was also the base for the mothers' meetings which she set up. She formed local branches of the YWCA and the Band of Hope, started a lending library, built a community hall and organised a medical mission to provide women doctors for Muslim women in India.

Some of Grisell's projects are unfashionable today. The Band of Hope, for example, was a branch of the temperance movement. But alcohol addiction was the drug problem of the day and the traditional song 'Oh Johnny my man' gives a vivid picture of it:

> *Oh Johnny my man, d'ye no think on risin'?*
> *The day is weel spent and the nicht's comin' on*

> *Yer siller's all dane*   (money, gone)
> *and the stoup's toom before ye*   (tankard, empty)
> *So rise up my Johnny, and come awa' hame...*

> *The bairnies at hame are roarin' and greetin'*   (children)
> *Nae meal in the barrel to fill their wee wames*   (stomachs)
> *You sit there drinkin' and leave us lamentin'*
> *So rise up my Johnny and come awa' hame.*[25]

The temperance movement is sometimes thought of as a church-led phenomenon. In fact, it grew out of the working class politics of the 1840s. The Church of Scotland hung back from it for over thirty years, earning it the nickname the 'Whisky Kirk' from its critics.[26] Grisell was part of the first wave of Church of Scotland involvement. Throughout her life, she kept up a daily rhythm of personal and family prayer, together with Robert and other members of the household. She died just four years into her deaconate. Soon afterwards, the Deaconess Hospital was opened in memory of her in Edinburgh. It provided health care for one of the poorest parts of the city as well as training women to be nurses and medical missionaries.

Other places associated with Grisell Baillie can be seen all along the route between here and St Boswells: Maxpoffle, where she nursed her elderly mother, was on the site of the present Maxpoffle House by the Bowden burn. In Newtown St Boswells, she had the Baillie Memorial Hall built in memory of her brother. With 'total abstinence' written into its conditions of use, it is no longer used as a community hall but was once the main venue for gatherings in Newtown.

Newtown St Boswells

Newtown St Boswells is not, in fact, all that new. It has been on the map for at least 300 years, and Neuton, 'the new farm' mentioned in the Charter book of Dryburgh Abbey, 1150, may well be the same place. It expanded greatly during the mid-19th century when trains first came to the Borders and soon became an important railway junction. This brought new life to the area in a number of ways. Sheep and cattle could now be brought to market by train instead of on the hoof and Newtown became famous for its stock sales. Also, in the early days, large numbers of workers were required to build the railway. Many of these were Irish men, some with their families, escaping from the potato famine. Others were Gaelic-speaking Scots dispossessed by the Highland Clearances.[27]

There are no trains left in the Borders today. The east-coast line still passes through Berwick, but the last of the inland routes closed in 1969. This is still bitterly regretted by many Borderers. Overnight, communications became difficult without a car. Workers from as far south as Hawick used to go dancing in Edinburgh on a Saturday night. More seriously perhaps, trains carried produce from the Borders to ports and markets all over Britain. It was said at the time that the loss of the railways would be bad for the local economy and in the 1990s the rising tide of job losses has lent weight to the campaign to have the Waverley line re-opened from Edinburgh to Carlisle, to increase the job opportunities and make the area more attractive to inward investment.

The Glen Road

Between Newtown and the Tweed, the path runs through a little glen, still following the Bowden burn. Here you pass through a fragment of ancient woodland, on a site which has been wooded since Cuthbert's time. There's a rich growth of moss and lichen on the trees and if you know your wild flowers, look out for wild garlic, dog's mercury, sanicle and 'townhall clock' – all indicators of ancient woodland. Even surer signs are some of the tiny flightless beetles. You may not notice them but, collectively, they take thousands of years to move from one area to another and are completely wiped out if a wood is destroyed. In spring and early summer, the loudest singing in the glen comes from the tiny wrens

– confident and supremely musical with a ratchety-sounding 'chur-rrr' a few notes from the end. You may also see bullfinches, treecreepers and various kinds of warblers. Occasionally, otters have been seen in the burn.

St Cuthbert and the otters

Ebba, Abbess of Coldingham, once invited Cuthbert to spend a few days with her community of monks and nuns on St Abb's Head. The monastery was going through troubled times. It had become more like a comfortable residential hotel than a working monastery and most of the community had largely given up any kind of spiritual life. As long as the food was top-quality, as long as the company was pleasant and the clothes fashionable, they were happy. It was rather like the royal court where St Ebba and many of her companions had grown up. Oratories had been made into parlours and there was a whiff of seduction in the air.[28] This may sound rather exciting to modern ears but it was not Ebba's idea of the religious life. Maybe she recognised a shallow self-centredness in their situation and the need to reconnect with a deeper reality. So she invited Cuthbert to come and speak to them and stay for a while.

Bede does not record what he said, but at least one man remembered what he did. In the middle of the night, apparently, he got up and slipped out of the monastery. One of the brothers saw him go. He followed him, thinking, perhaps, that the saintly visitor was up to no good, that he was a hypocrite. Cuthbert followed the cliff path down to the beach. The brother watched from behind a rock as Cuthbert waded far out into the sea and stood there for the rest of the night, with the waves lapping round him.[29] At dawn he came out and knelt down on the sand to pray. Suddenly, two otters came scampering up the beach and rolled on the ground by his feet. It was as if they were trying to warm him with their breath and dry him with their fur. After a while, he blessed them and they slipped back into the water.[30]

Nowadays, we're likely to be charmed by this story but the spy behind the rock was afraid. To him, it was a glimpse of the restored innocence of creation, something he had been disinclined to believe in. His own suspicious mind had found him out and he felt wretched. Also, he thought Cuthbert would be furious when he found out that he had been spied on. He need not have worried. Like Jesus in the Gospels, Cuthbert had no time for the sort of hero-worship which people cultivated round about him. He simply asked the man not to tell anyone and that was that.

Parts of this story may be exaggerated, but the general idea is clear enough. Many of us are prisoners of comfort today. Our economies are founded on ever-expanding markets, high energy consumption and a global trade in luxury goods, though we know that the planet cannot sustain that kind of growth indefinitely. The story of Cuthbert and the otters speaks directly to that situation: by practising non-attachment to personal comfort and being open to God in prayer, he becomes the kind of person whom the rest of creation can genuinely respect.

The Glen Road makes an excellent short walk for people who can walk up to one mile (total) and manage a flight of steps. Not suitable for wheelchairs. Limited parking possible at Newtown end, next to the Treatment Works. Fairly level unsurfaced path with one steep hill. 16 shallow steps. Can be slippery in wet weather. Seat near beginning and again at the end. It's possible to make this a shorter walk by doing it in one direction only, but you would need to arrange for someone to collect you by car at the Dryburgh end. There is a seat just above the collection point, in case you need to wait, and steps to negotiate on the way down.

Tweed Horizons

From the top of the steps, the path runs along the perimeter fence of Tweed Horizons. This Centre for Sustainable Technology houses small businesses which try to combine economic viability with better stewardship of the earth. It's an experimental project which calls for a great deal of imagination and ingenuity. Tweed Horizons shares ideas with similar centres overseas through video-conferencing, hosts educational events and runs demonstration projects. Their combined heat and power plant, for example, produces very little waste and runs off local forestry by-products and fast-growing willows which are harvested in the grounds. An organic gardening business operates from here too. If you hear the quacking of ducks, that's the slug-control unit at work.

The original parts of the white-towered building were constructed in the 1930s as a junior seminary for a Catholic missionary order known as the White Fathers. The order began in Algeria and was very poor at first. Unable to buy traditional European habits, they wore the ordinary clothes of local Algerian men – the white *gandoura*. This might be seen as a radical thing to do. Missionaries who wear local dress nowadays often do so as a sign of solidarity and respect. Sadly, perhaps, the White Fathers reverted to European habits as soon as they could afford them. St Columba's Seminary, as it was called, provided an education for boys up to the age of 16, some of whom went on to join the order. In the early 1970s, the seminary was taken over by Strathclyde Regional Council and became St Columba's School, providing rural experiences for city kids. Living in community was an important experience for them too. Whole classes came, together with their teachers, working, praying and playing together as well as exploring the countryside.

The chain bridge, Dryburgh

The path drops down to the Tweed next to an old suspension bridge known as the chain bridge. Dryburgh village, across the river, is four miles from Newtown by road, so the bridge provides a useful shortcut. Before it was built, there was a ferry service here, but this could be dangerous when the river was in spate. An earlier footbridge was damaged in a storm and washed away. Grisell Baillie (p.72) saw to the building of this one in 1872 when she was living in Dryburgh Abbey House. St Cuthbert's Way does not actually cross the bridge but it is worth going as far as the half-way point to enjoy the view. Old Melrose is less than two miles upstream from here. Monksford, an older crossing place, is just out of sight around the bend in the same direction. Pilgrims travelling between St Cuthbert's Chapel at Old Melrose and Dryburgh Abbey would probably have used the crossing at Monksford. Whether it was in use in Cuthbert's day is an open question, but this stretch of the river would certainly have been known to him. In summer, look out for two different kinds of wagtails by the bridge: pied wagtails in classic black and white and their more flighty cousins, the grey wagtails, tumbling for insects from flat stones near the bank. Check out those primrose-yellow underparts.

Carved stone basin from Dryburgh Abbey

Dryburgh Abbey

Dryburgh Abbey is just five minutes' walk from the village on the other side of the bridge. It's the most tranquil of the Border abbeys today and is surrounded by mature trees, including some magnificent cedars. The chapter house has a wonderful acoustic and baptisms are still held there occasionally. There's a dawn service every year in the abbey grounds on Easter morning. You might like to take a detour to the abbey, but only do so if you have plenty of energy in reserve, as the path between the chain bridge and St Boswells can be demanding with lots of steps. It can also be very muddy.

Dryburgh Abbey was founded by an Anglo-Norman couple: Hugh de Morville and Beatrice de Beauchamp. The clergy were brought from Alnwick and were Premonstratensians, originally from France. One of the most intriguing parts of the abbey is the vault known as St Modan's Chapel next to the church. St Modan has no obvious connection with the Premonstratensians. Modan is an Irish name and there are at least four St Modans in the old calendars of saints. One late report, written in 1631, claims that Modan was the Abbot of Dryburgh in 522 and was the same St Modan who worked in the Falkirk, Dumbarton and Gare Loch areas at some other time in his life.[31] No good historian likes an eleven-hundred-year gap, but if there is any truth at all in this tradition, we could be looking at an Irish missionary who was in Dryburgh over a century before Aidan arrived on Lindisfarne and almost fifty years before Columba landed on Iona. Where could he have come from? The earliest surviving signs of Christianity in Scotland come from Galloway, especially around Whithorn and Kirkmadrine, and there is a later tradition that some time during the sixth century a group of students came from Ireland to study at Whithorn, but there is no contemporary evidence for this.[32]

However, there are signs of Christianity in the Borders before Aidan's mission. These are mainly, perhaps entirely, among the Britons. In the Ettrick Valley, in the late fifth/early sixth century, someone carved a little praying figure with bare feet and short-cropped hair, wearing a knee-length tunic marked with an equal-armed cross. His arms are bent at the elbow and his hands raised in prayer, in a gesture still used by some people today. There is no name on the stone. He could have been a hermit, a missionary or the leader of a local Christian community. All we know for sure is that he was remembered and honoured by someone. In the early sixth century, an inexperienced stone-mason carved the names of two brothers, Nudus and Dumnogenus, on a memorial stone in the Yarrow Valley. He carved them clumsily but in Latin, suggesting at the very least a Christian education, so it's possible that he and the two brothers were already Christians. In a field nearby, eight stone-lined cists were found, aligned east-west, without gravegoods. This too suggests Christian burial. And just over the hill, other memorial stones from the same period have been found in the Peebles area.[33] The place-name Eccles (p.122) in Berwickshire comes from the old Brittonic word for 'church', so there were probably British Christians there before the time of Cuthbert and Aidan.[34]

St Modan could conceivably come from this early period, but

there's another, more likely, possibility. 'Modan' may well be 'Aidan' with an 'm' prefix: Mo-Aedan – 'my Aidan'.[35] Other Irish saints' names behave in similar ways: Lasair and Molaise for example, are generally thought to have been the same person. Old Melrose was founded during Aidan's lifetime and it seems reasonable to assume that he visited the area at least once during his 16 years on Lindisfarne. Perhaps a church or outlying chapel was dedicated in his honour.

Dryburgh Abbey: No reserved parking places. Car park in grounds of Dryburgh Abbey Hotel (for use of guests) is closer to the ticket office – 40 yds from car park to office, surface level, hard-packed gravel, 6 ft wide. Distance from main car/coach park to ticket office: about 100yds, paved, level, 4 ft wide, no rail or seats. Once past the ticket office you are already into very pleasant grounds and can see the abbey across the lawn. Distance from ticket office to entrance to abbey church: 180 yds. Surface – paved for first 150 yds, then small gravel chips, gradient level-slight, width 6 ft. Benches (March–November only) at 40 yds and 75 yds. One picnic table. Inside abbey church: surface slightly uneven paving stones. One shallow step over a low wall, benches. Nave to cloister – 10 steps down, no rail. Nave to dormitory – 18 steps up, rail part of way. There is an alternative route into the cloister but it involves 11 steps up. Benches in cloister. Path round outside of abbey buildings – small-medium gravel, gradient one steep stretch, then moderate to level, 10 ft wide, no rails or seats. All gates wide enough for wheelchairs. Toilet in main car park – one step up, standard.

Approaching St Boswells

According to local tradition, a hermit once lived at Hare Craig or Crag, after the Holmes Burn footbridge, but nothing more is known about him or her.[36] The next bridge crosses the West Burn just below the village. At one time, this was a well-used path as people used to collect drinking-water from the Dreepin' Well (Dripping Well) on the bank. There's little trace of it today. By the 19th century the burn was heavily polluted from the houses above and there was also concern about the well. Piped water was introduced in 1869 and this reduced the risk of cholera and other diseases, but it was 1892 before a basic sewage system was installed. Amazingly, there was local opposition. The innovators were branded 'hi-jeanies' and when the Council tried to introduce refuse collections in 1896 and 1900 there were further protests. Ashpits at the back door had 'aye been' and some rate-payers complained about the expense.[37]

St Boswells

St Boswells is named after Boisil, St Cuthbert's Irish mentor and a saint in his own right. He's best remembered as a scripture scholar but he was also a prophet – that is, a person of special insight and understanding. Prophecy is sometimes thought of simply as supernatural knowledge of the future, but there can be natural explanations for it as well. It's possible that after a week studying with Cuthbert and being tended by him in his last illness, Boisil had a clear sense of where this young person's gifts and talents lay and was able to 'unfold' his future to him. In other words, he helped Cuthbert to understand himself and where his life might be heading.

St Boswells village was called Lesudden till relatively recently.[38] St Boswells was the name of the parish and the parish church. Within living memory, a fair known as St Boswells Fair was held every year on July 18th on St Boswells Green, at the entrance to the village. Originally it was held on the feast of St Boisil as part of the holy-day celebrations at old St Boisil's church (p.86). It was still going in the first half of the 20th century with sales of sheep, cattle and especially horses, side-shows and 'shuggy boats' (swings) for the children. Gypsies and other Travellers came from all over Scotland, Ireland and England for the fair and camped on the Green with their carts and caravans, horses and lurchers. It used to be a great occasion for the whole community but only Travellers celebrate it now, largely among themselves.[39]

In the public hall opposite the post office, Grisell Baillie held a sale of work and Fair-Day Tea (with strawberries and cream) in aid of her 'Zezana' mission to women in India. Along from the hall, on Jenny Moore's Road, there used to be two fields known as the Cuddy fields. It's often said that the element 'cud' or 'cuddy' in a place-name shows some connection with St Cuthbert: Kirkcudbright, for example, Cuthbert's Church. But we need to be careful about this. Local historian Jean Lawrie knew exactly how the Cuddy fields got their name. That was where Johnnie the Cuddy lived when she was a little girl. 'Cuddy' is also Scots for a donkey, pony or horse.[40] The church next to the hall was originally dedicated to St Modan and is usually open during the week. The 'dove window' by Liz Rowley celebrates the joy and freedom of the Holy Spirit in colours of fire and air. It makes an interesting contrast with the more static-looking figures round about.

Just before you turn left into Braehead Road, you see on the other side of the street one of the outlets for the 'new' public water supply which replaced the Dreepin' Well and others. A quarter of the world's population still has no access to safe drinking water, even from outlets like these.[41] The text written above the tap is taken from the story of the woman at the well in John's Gospel: 'Whosoever drinketh of this water shall thirst again; but whosoever drinketh of the water that I shall give him shall never thirst'.[42] It's a beautiful verse but I can't help thinking it sounds a little grudging in a situation like this. Some Victorians believed that improvements to public health and well-being were likely to distract people from more spiritual things. Perhaps there was such a person on the water committee.

Notes

1   The Royal Commission on the Ancient Monuments of Scotland, *An Inventory of the Ancient and Historical Monuments of Roxburghshire*, Vol.2, Edinburgh, 1956, 317–8

2   op.cit. 319. The depiction of the Campestres is known from other sites.

3   Noel Dermot O'Donoghue, *The Mountain Behind the Mountain*, Edinburgh, 1993, 39–45; Mary Low, *Celtic Christianity and Nature*, Edinburgh, 1996, 29, 43–5.

4   Anne Ross, *Pagan Celtic Britain*, revised edition, London, 1992, 45–93. Mary Low, op. cit. 59–62.

5   J. Curle, *A Roman Frontier Post and its People*, 1911, p.113. For a complete inventory from the first excavations, see Curle, 103–139.

6   Personal communication, 22 May 1998.

7   Bede, *Life* 15; She is often known simply as Hildmer's wife. Neither Bede nor the Anonymous tell us her name, but 'Eadswith' is written in the margin of three of the early manuscripts. Colgrave, *Two Lives*, 347.

8   Maxwell Jones, medical superintendent 1962–9, interviewed 1983. For this and what follows, see Liz Findlay, *Dingleton 1872–98*, unpublished dissertation, 1998, Dingleton Archive, Melrose.

9   John Dent and Rory McDonald, *Early Settlers in the Borders*, Scottish Borders Council, Melrose, 1997, 65–7

10   Ian Armit, *Celtic Scotland*, London, 1997, 50–3. For a full survey see J.S. Rideout, O.A. Owen, E. Halpin, *Hillforts of Southern Scotland*, Edinburgh, 1992.

11   Bede, *EH* 5.12; Low, *Celtic Christianity and Nature*, 6–9, 43–5; Nora Chadwick, *Poetry and Prophecy*, Cambridge, 1942; Ronald Black suggests that the Otherworld under the Eildons was known to Thomas from local Cumbric, i.e. Brittonic, lore. Paper presented at 11th International Congress of Celtic Studies, Cork, 1999.

12   Walter Scott, *The Lay of the Last Minstrel*, ed. George Gilfillan, Edinburgh, 1857, p.127. The friar's comment appears in James Hogg's version of the story, where there are three demons instead of one and the feat is part of a contest between the friar and Michael Scot. *The Three Perils of Man*, ed. Matthew McDiarmid, Edinburgh, 173–204. 'Fair ta'en on wi' his-sel' means foolishly proud of himself.

13   Dante, *The Divine Comedy*, canto XX, lines 115–117.

14   Anthony Pym, 'Twelfth-century Toledo and strategies of the literalist Trojan horse', *Target*, 6:1, 1994, 44.

15   Pym, op.cit. 44–50

16   Jose S. Gil, *La Escuela de Traductores de Toledo y los Colaboradores Judios*, Toledo, 1985, 53, n.218. This was a translation from a work by the great Muslim scholar Averroës or Ibn Rushd, based on Aristotle's *De Historia Animalibus*.

17   When a group of unruly barons went on the rampage in 1236, the Chronicler wrote that they were like fish, 'who (as Aristotle states in his fourth book upon Animals) devour whatever they can catch.' Stephenson, *CM*, 1263.

18   Bowden Village Committee, *Bowden*, Galashiels, 1989, 2–4.

19   J.S.M. Macdonald, *Bowden Kirk 1128–1978*, Hawick, 1978.

20   *Dictionary of Scottish Church History and Theology (DSCHT)*, 778.

21   Macdonald, *Bowden Kirk*, 8–9.

22   Luke 1.78.

23 D.P.Thomson, 'Scotland's First Deaconess', in *Women of the Scottish Church* III, The Border Booklets, National Library of Scotland.

24 Countess Ashburnham, *Lady Grisell Baillie*, Edinburgh, 1893.

25 This street song, common in the mid 19th century, was collected by Robert Ford in *Vagabond Songs and Ballads*, publ. Alex Gardner, Paisley, 1904; recorded by Jean Redpath on 'Song of the Seals', Philo Records Inc., 1977.

26 *DSCHT*, 815–6.

27 Walter Elliot, 'The Burghs, Towns and Villages' in *BB*, 178.

28 Bede, *EH* 5.25.

29 Like Drythelm in the Tweed at Old Melrose. See p.60.

30 Bede, *Life* 10.

31 A.P. Forbes, *Kalendars of Scottish Saints*, Edinburgh, 1872, 400–402, citing Cemararius, *De Scotorum Fortitudine*, Paris, 1631.

32 One of these students was St Finnian or Uiniau of Moville. See also Cuthbert section, note 53. Parts of the story are told in Middle-Irish which did not develop till the end of the ninth century. J.H. Bernard and R. Atkinson, *The Irish Liber Hymnorum*,Henry Bradshaw Society, 1898, I.22. For a more accessible edition, see John and Winifred McQueen, *St Nynia*, Edinburgh, 1990, 41–3. For more on the Irish connection, see P.A. Wilson, 'St Ninian and Candida Casa: Literary Evidence from Ireland', *Transactions of the Dumfries and Galloway Natural History and Antiquarian Society* 41, 1964, 156–85.

33 John Baldwin, *Exploring Scotland's Heritage: Lothian and the Borders*, Edinburgh, 1985, 100–101, 124–5. The Praying Man of Ettrick, known as 'the Overkirkhope Orans' after the farm where the stone was found, is now on display in the new Museum of Scotland in Edinburgh.

34 G.W.S. Barrow, 'The Childhood of Christianity in Scotland: a Note on Some Place-Name Evidence', *Scottish Studies* 27, 1983, 1–15. Simon Taylor, 'Place names and the early church in Scotland', *Records of the Scottish Church History Society*, XXVIII, 3–4.

35 Simon Taylor, personal communication, 19.6.98.

36 Jean S. Lawrie, *Old St Boswells*, St Boswells, 1974, 40.

37 Lawrie, op.cit. 49–52.

38 It was still marked as such on the six-inch Ordnance Survey map, 1863.

39 Lawrie, op.cit. 11–14.

40 op.cit.13–14, 38. The fair-day teas started in 1882 and continued annually till the Great War of 1914–18.

41 Water Aid, One World News Service, March 1998.

42 From the story of Jesus and the woman at the well. John 4.5–42.

St Boswells to Harestanes

Towards Mertoun Bridge

From St Boswells the path follows the river along the side of the golf course and on towards Mertoun Bridge. Just before you get there, there's an old mill with a cauld (weir) in front of it. You can sometimes see salmon leap here, especially in spring and autumn. Wild salmon have a precarious existence these days, and the Tweed is very important to them, as it is to the general ecology of the area. A fish symbol-stone, possibly representing a salmon, can still be seen at Borthwick Mains, a few miles south-west of Hawick. It may be early Christian and/or Pictish and dates from the sixth or seventh century.[1] In Gaelic literature, the salmon is a symbol of wisdom and was probably sacred in pre-Christian Celtic tradition. Later, Christian poets like Giolla Brighde Mac Con Midhe, used it as an image for Christ: 'the bright blessed graceful salmon' and 'the salmon of the well of mercy'.[2]

Psalms and hymns

The anonymous Life of Cuthbert gives us a tiny glimpse of a musical procession along the banks of the Tweed.[3] Cuthbert had been invited to the village of a man called Sibba who lived somewhere beside the river. He arrived 'with a company of people', singing as they walked. This was not just a quick burst of song. We're told that they sang several 'psalms and hymns' so they were probably heard long before they were seen. Psalms were part of the daily rhythm of life in medieval monasteries. These ancient pre-Christian hymns spoke so directly to human experience that they were adopted into Christianity and are still sung all over the world, by Christians and Jews. The hymns would have been in Latin but it's possible that Cuthbert already knew some in his own everyday language. A few years later, in 680, a herdsman called Caedmon would begin composing beautiful hymns in Old English, much to everyone's surprise, including his own. Caedmon was one of those people who are convinced that they can't sing. Whenever party-pieces were called for, he would quietly disappear. One night after this happened, he went out to the byre to feed the beasts and fell asleep there. A man came to him in his dreams, called him by name and asked him for a song. 'I don't know how to sing,' said Caedmon, 'that's why I left the feast.' 'But you shall sing for me,' said the man. 'What shall I sing about?' 'Sing about the Creation of things,' said the man. And Caedmon began to sing – in his own voice – a song he had never heard before.[4]

St Boswells' 'auld kirk'

This is about a mile beyond Mertoun Bridge in Benrig cemetery. Only the foundations are visible today, in the field on your right, after the steep flight of steps up from the river. This is certainly an early burial ground and local tradition associates it with Boisil himself. There used to be a village here, the original St Boswells. The original St Boswells fair took place here too, on the 'haugh' – the area between the river bank and the higher ground. No one knows for certain whether Boisil did actually found a church here, but it's within easy reach of Old Melrose and Bede tells us that when Cuthbert went out preaching and teaching in the towns and villages round about, he was following Boisil's example.[5] The next burn you cross is called St Boswells Burn. A flight of steps takes you up from there towards Maxton church on the outskirts of Maxton village.

Maxton church

'St Cuthbert's Church of Mackistun' first appears in the records some 500 years after the time of Cuthbert, but like St Boswells' auld kirk, it could well have been served from Old Melrose, maybe even by Cuthbert himself. Maxton has (or had) another Cuthbert connection only a short distance away. Till the 1960s, there was a St Cuthbert's Well at the west end of the village, but it was tarred over in a road-improvement project and is now completely untraceable. In the late 12th century, Maxton was officially linked to Melrose Abbey. The landowner gave the monks pasture for a hundred sheep, twelve oxen, six cows, three horses and a sow, as well as the right to cut peat and quarry stone. Maxton church is still used today but is usually locked during the week. If you want to go inside, a key can be collected from Elm Cottage, the house on the left at the top of the lane. One of the more unusual features inside is the Hebrew inscription half way up the wall. It reads: 'Blessed are the people that know the joyful sound' and 'Come let us worship and bow down'. These are both quotes from the book of Psalms and were carved here during the 18th century.[6] The first may have been composed originally for a festival and 'Come let us worship... ' has been used for centuries as a traditional beginning to morning prayer. All the saints of Lindisfarne and the Borders would have known both of these off by heart, as would Jesus himself.

St John Duns Scotus

There's a tradition that the great Franciscan philosopher John Duns Scotus (c.1266–1308) was born in the parish of Maxton. However, it is now more or less certain that he came from Duns, about twenty miles from here: all the earliest manuscripts call him John of Duns and the Maxton version comes from an 18th-century manuscript notorious for its mistakes and downright inventions.[23] If we can salvage anything for Maxton, it may be that he had relatives here, but whether he did or not, the Tweed, the Cheviot and the stories of St Cuthbert would all have been familiar to him. Most of his adult life was spent abroad. He taught in Oxford, Cambridge, Paris and Cologne and was known as the 'subtle doctor' because of the intricacy of his thought. In spite of this, he had a deep conviction that love was more important than reason, in the mind of God. Not everyone agreed with him and he was a controversial figure (the word 'dunce' is said to have been coined from his name) as well as an influential one. He was declared a saint in 1993.

Dere Street

Soon after Maxton, St Cuthbert's Way follows the line of Dere Street for several miles. This was a Roman military road. It was built between about AD 79 and 83 on the orders of Agricola, general and imperial governor, who had conquered Wales and the North of England and now had his sights set on the Caledonians. He would eventually build forts as far north as Dunkeld in Perthshire, but back in the Mediterranean world, something was happening the significance of which he would not have believed. A book was circulating and some letters and stories about a Jewish carpenter-turned-rabbi, executed by the governor of Palestine in the reign of Tiberius.

The book was Mark's Gospel, the letters were St Paul's and the stories were being collected into two new Gospels, Matthew and Luke, at around the same time as the slaves and engineers were working on Dere Street. John's Gospel had yet to be written. No doubt Agricola would have heard of the *Christiani* but it's unlikely that he took them very seriously. He probably saw them as that small middle-eastern sect which had been held responsible for the great fire in Rome nearly twenty years earlier. Some of the ringleaders had been executed around that time, including two Jews, Peter and Paul. Pockets of *Christiani* still existed here and there but Agricola was not in the business of rooting them out. 'Love God and your neighbour as yourself' hardly had the same ring about it as Caesar's '*Veni Vidi Vici*': 'I came, I saw, I conquered.'[8] He would have been surprised to hear that, as a blueprint for living, it has survived empires and all kinds of human folly, including, often, the folly of Christians.

Lilyot's Cross

Walkers with a taste for the gruesome may enjoy a short diversion to Lilliard's Stone. The inscription on it, about the courage of Maid Lilliard and her horrific injuries, has provoked, variously, admiration, revulsion and fits of laughter. Fortunately perhaps, she never existed. Her 'epitaph' is a piece of doggerel based on a truly awful version of the English Border ballad 'Chevy Chase' in which the wounded soldier is a man and the conflict is the battle of Otterburn (1388).[9] No doubt women were sometimes caught up in Border warfare, but Lilliard's last stand at the battle of Ancrum Moor (1545) is pure fiction. The name existed long before the legend grew up around it. Lilliard's or Lilyot's Cross was a traditional meeting place where boundary disputes were decided in the 14th century.[10] These meetings took place on 'march days' ('march' meaning 'boundary') and usually involved the Wardens of the Marches, leaders of local families whose job it was to settle disputes and bring offenders to justice. The names Percy and Douglas crop up frequently at this period. They could also involve some major political and religious figures from outside.

The Bishops of Durham and Carlisle were here in 1373 'to correct offenders against the truces'. Five years later there was an international summit meeting between the Earl of Carrick, heir to the Scottish throne, and John of Gaunt, uncle of the English king, Richard II. Arguments were sometimes decided by single combat, and crowds gathered to watch the spectacle and be ready for the outcome. The Wardens met regularly, but some of these more important meetings were linked with religious festivals: the feast of St John the Baptist for example, the Monday after Trinity Sunday, the feast of St Peter and St Paul or the feast of St Martin of Tours.[11] Human attempts at government were believed to reflect God's way for the world, however dimly.

Border warfare

When Cuthbert walked along Dere Street, he was already walking a boundary of sorts. Before the Anglo-Saxon invasions, it lay between two old British kingdoms. By the sixth century, new Anglian settlements were appearing to the east, under the protection of the royal house at Bamburgh.[12] Soon they would control the whole of south-east Scotland all the way up to Edinburgh. Beyond that were the Picts and the Scots. When their king, Kenneth mac Alpin, burned down the remains of Old Melrose in AD 839 (p.62) he was invading an area which had been under Anglian control for some 300 years.

His successors kept up the pressure and in 973 Lothian and the Borders were formally ceded to the Scots in exchange for tribute. Malcolm II completed the process by his victory at Carham in 1018 and, gradually, the present Scotland–England border came into being. It was much disputed, but such changes as followed were mostly temporary. When the Anglo-Saxons were defeated by the Normans in 1066, the Scots faced a powerful new neighbour in the south. Norman influence in Scotland was complete by the reign of David I (1124–53). David, youngest son of Malcolm III and Margaret, had spent the whole of his adolescence at the Anglo-Norman court; his sister Matilda was married to the English king, Henry I; and David himself was Earl of Huntingdon and Northamptonshire as well as younger brother of the King of Scots. It was Henry who obtained lands for Earl David in the Scottish Borders and David who invited many of his Anglo-Norman friends to settle there, among them two families who would eventually become kings of Scotland: Stewart and De Brus.[13]

Scotland often had to struggle to remain independent. In 1296, Edward I of England mounted a successful invasion. Eighteen years later, the wagons of his son, Edward II, trundled along Dere Street on their way to defeat at the hands of Robert the Bruce. In the mid-1540s, the armies of Henry VIII passed this way during the 'rough wooing', the attempt to force the infant Mary, Queen of Scots, into marriage with Henry's son. The battle of Ancrum Moor was part of the same campaign.[14] The 'wooing' failed but it brought devastation to the Borders. According to one account, 243 villages were destroyed, along with five market towns, 16 castles and tower houses, 13 mills, seven religious houses and three 'spitals', i.e. pilgrim hostels-cum-hospitals.[15] All the great Border abbeys were destroyed. As for the 243 villages, no accounts survive of what happened there.

Raiders and reivers

People on both sides of the border survived as best they could. The fighting did not go on continually and some places were affected more badly than others, but with harvests lost and houses burned some people became expert at less peaceable activities such as cattle-thieving, free-booting and preying on their neighbours. By the 16th century, all these were specialities of the Border reivers. Nowadays, the Border Reivers is the name of the district rugby team. Then, reivers were not exactly outlaws, nor were they the poor and the dispossessed. They might be farmers, soldiers or gentry some of the time, reivers at other times. Family loyalty was intense and blood-feud a matter of honour and duty, though families could also be divided amongst themselves.

The main reiver families on the Middle March were Kerrs and Scotts with Fenwicks facing them across the border. To the east on the Scottish side, there were Humes and Pringles; to the west, Elliots, Armstrongs, Rutherfords, Grahams, Maxwells, Douglases and so on. Between them, there was a shifting pattern of alliances, both in relation to each other and to national politics.[16] Only when the situation began to be resolved between the two countries did reiving come to an end. In 1603, Queen Elizabeth I of England died, leaving the throne to her nearest relative, King James VI of Scotland, and the United Kingdom of Great Britain came into existence for the first time. That was not the end of hostilities however. Covenanters and Royalists fought here in the 17th century.[17] Even after a common parliament was set up in 1707, Jacobite armies passed through the Borders on their way south in 1715 and 1745. A little girl on an errand from Ancrum to Jedburgh is said to have run into a column of them on the march and been protected by a 'bonnie gentleman' on a horse. This turned out to be none other than Charles Edward Stuart, 'Bonnie Prince Charlie' himself. Others were not so lucky. Adam Duncanson, laird of Maxpoffle, buried his money in the woods and was murdered by a party of Jacobite soldiers for refusing to reveal its whereabouts. His ghost is still said to haunt the glen.[18]

Today, relations between Scotland and England are changing once again. Whichever way the future lies, the past holds few attractions around here. In the words of an 18th-century song, adapted and recorded by Dick Gaughan, one of Scotland's leading living songwriters:

Let the love of our land's sacred rights
To the love of our people succeed
Let friendship and honour unite
And flourish on both sides the Tweed.[19]

St Cuthbert's Way crosses the B6400 between Harestanes Visitor Centre and Monteviot House. The village of Ancrum is about one mile to the east, beyond Harestanes. Seen from the A68, Ancrum does not look particularly inviting, but the centre is pretty with its village green, market cross and some old 18th-century houses. Overnight accommodation is available. Refreshments depend on pub and shop opening hours.

Harestanes
The countryside centre at Harestanes (10am–5pm, April to

October) provides a base for woodland walks on Lothian Estate and specialises in books, exhibitions and information about the countryside. It has an excellent tearoom with homebaking and ice-cream and a games room upstairs. It's a favourite destination for families, the highlight being the adventure playground for younger children. One of the lesser-known images in the Hebrew Bible is the little girl who, in the Book of Proverbs, plays at God's feet as the world is being created. Some translations disguise her by call-ing her a 'master craftsman' or a 'builder' but what she represents is the wisdom of God, known in Greek as Sophia, whose first activity is to play and delight in creation:

> *The Lord created me the beginning of all his works*
> *before all else that he made, long ago...*
> *When he set the heavens in their place I was there,*
> *when he girdled the ocean with the horizon,*
> *when he fixed the canopy of clouds overhead*
> *and set the springs of ocean firm in their place*
> *when he prescribed the limits for the sea*
> *and knit together earth's foundations.*
> *Then I was at his side each day,*
> *his darling and his delight,*
> *playing on the earth, when he had finished it,*
> *while my delight was in mankind.* [20]

Other biblical writers focus on God as law-giver, judge, guardian, shepherd, father, mother, rock, light, and so on. The child-image is unusual and even in Proverbs is distanced a little from God, as if the writer hesitated to compare God too directly with a child at play. On the whole, most people prefer to meditate on grown-up images of God – and it's easy to understand why. But I can't help thinking that perhaps we have lost the connection between wisdom and playfulness. We tend to think of them as opposites: wisdom as serene and elderly; play as childish and messy. But the expression 'all work and no play makes Jack a dull boy' reminds us that play, re-creation, is good for tired adults as well.

Two dedicated parking spaces on paved area within 50 yds of the door to the Centre. Further parking nearby. Approach level, with level-entry doors. Tiled floors inside throughout. Shop, café and exhibition area all accessible. Seats in café. Indoor play area is upstairs. No lift. Paved courtyard at the back with picnic tables. Accessible toilet, open same hours as Centre. 'Wheelchair-accessible' woodland trail – about one mile (total). Surface hard-packed gravel. Pond near Centre with level viewing platform. Adventure playground grassy and uneven. No special facilities for children with special needs, but includes swings and accessible Play House.

Notes

1   Baldwin, *Lothian and the Borders*, 101, 125.

2   Low, *Celtic Christianity and Nature*, 76–78.

3   Anon. 7; Colgrave, *Two Lives*, 121.

4   Bede, *EH* 4. 24.

5   *EH* 4.27.

6   Psalm 89.15 and Psalm 95.6.

7   Charles Balic, *John Duns Scotus*, Rome, 1966, 5–9, 16–24.; Henry Docherty, 'The Brockie Forgeries', *Innes Review*, 16, 1965, 79–127.

8   Mk.12.30–31; Julius Caesar, *On the Gallic War*, 3.7.2.

9   The inscription reads: 'Fair Maiden Lilliard lies under this stane/Little was her stature, but muckle was her fame/Upon the English loons she laid many thumps/And when her legs were cuttit off, she fought upon her stumps.' Cf. the death of Witherington in the 17th-century broadside version of 'Chevy Chase': 'For when his legs were smitten off/He fought upon his stumps.' S.C. Wilson, 'A Border Meeting Place: Lilyot's Cross', *Transactions of the Hawick Archeological Society*, 1926, 5–6. James Reed, *The Border Ballads*, London, 1973, 125.

10 Wilson, ibid.; George Ridpath, *The Border History of England and Scotland*, ed. Philip Ridpath, Berwick, 1848, 282.

11 Wilson, ibid.

12 Christopher D. Morris, 'The Early Historic Period' in Omand, *BB*, 56–61.

13 Michael Lynch, *Scotland: A New History*, London, 1995, 79–80.

14 Walter Elliot, 'The Burghs, Towns and Villages', *BB*, 176.

15   Report by the Earl of Hertford, quoted in George Ridpath, *The Border History of England and Scotland*, 1848, 287.

16   For a popular account of the Border reivers, see George MacDonald Fraser, *The Steel Bonnets*, London, 1971.

17   On 13th September 1645, a Covenanting force under General Alexander Leslie defeated the Royalist armies of the Marquis of Montrose just outside Selkirk at Philiphaugh. There was a particularly bloody massacre of camp followers afterwards, including large numbers of Irish and Highland women and children who had surrendered.

18   Douglas, *Roxburgh, Selkirk and Peebles*, 1899, 391–403; *History of Bowden District*, Bowden Women's Rural Institute, 1967, 7.

19   From the album 'Handful of Earth', Topic Records, 1989.

20   Proverbs 8. 22–31. New English Bible.

Harestanes to Morebattle

Monteviot House was built in the grounds of Ancrum Spital, a medieval hostel-cum-hospital run by the Church. There was also a chapel nearby and a burial ground. The present mansion dates from around 1830, though parts of it are slightly older.[1] It is not open to the public, though you can visit the gardens from 12–5pm, April to October. St Cuthbert's Way runs through the beautiful old woods behind the house, but it's possible that Dere Street followed the line of the main drive. If so, this would have been the last stage on Cuthbert's journey from Old Melrose to the Teviot (see below).

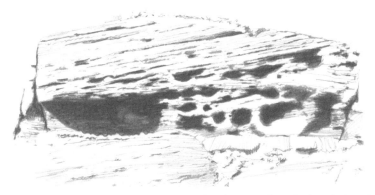

A weathered stone in the wall of Cessford Castle

Monteviot belongs to a branch of the Kerr family. One of their ancestors, William, third Earl of Lothian, was among the 'Lords Covenanters' who supported the Scottish parliament and the General Assembly against King Charles I. Charles was an autocratic ruler whose reign degenerated into civil war, both in Scotland and England. William was part of the Scottish parliamentary force which captured Newcastle in 1640 and spent a miserable winter there fighting Charles's forces. William's letters to his father at this time are full of requests for cheering luxuries: lace-trimmed slippers, a French barber, a good horse. 'A furr coat' would have been useful, he wrote, rather peevishly, but the weather was now improving; soon he would need a camp bed 'with quilts and a small bolster... but I would have it a pretty one and all fitted for carriage'.[2]

In return, his father asked for a shipload of coal and a fiddler. The fiddler could not be spared as he was also a soldier and was needed to fight. Also he was rarely sober. The coal, however, was eventually sent after much difficulty. The miners had fled and many of the pits were 'drouned and spoyld'.[3] Here we get a tiny glimpse of other lives 'spoyld' by war: miners without pits, a drunken fiddler. For the next twenty years, William trod an uncomfortable tight-rope between his Covenanting principles and his traditional respect for royalty. When Charles II came to the throne in 1660, William acknowledged his right to rule but refused to declare the Covenant illegal. He was fined £6,000.[4]

The White Fathers (p.77) lived at Monteviot for ten years before moving to their purpose-built school at St Columba's in 1958. The chapel they used was on the West Lawn but it was demolished in 1960 and a new chapel, the Chapel of the Border Saints, was created. It contains carvings of St Cuthbert, St Boisil, St John Duns Scotus and others. There is also a crucifix by George Wyllie. None of this is open to the public at present.

After Monteviot, St Cuthbert's Way crosses the River Teviot. If Cuthbert was heading for the Cheviots, he too would have crossed the river near here. Sometimes, however, he might have turned left, towards Kelso, Coldstream and Berwick – or right towards Hawick. In the 19th century, a Celtic handbell was found near Ednam, two miles from Kelso on the River Eden. It was of the kind used in early Irish and Pictish monasteries and was quickly dubbed 'St Cuthbert's Bell'. There's no evidence that it was in fact his, or even that it came originally from Ednam, but bells like this have been associated with Columban monasteries in Scotland, so a link with Old Melrose or Lindisfarne cannot be ruled out. No one paddling down the Tweed from Old Melrose can avoid passing the mouth of the Eden, with Ednam just a little way upstream.[5]

As for Hawick, St Cuthbert's Way goes nowhere near there today, but in the story of Cuthbert, the boy and the eagle (p.181) we are told that they were travelling south, along the banks of the Teviot. Since the river runs south-west to north-east, the writer's geography is a bit hazy here, but if we presume that he means south-west, then this must mean upstream towards Hawick. There was once a medieval chapel of St Cuthbert and an old burial ground at Slitrig near Hawick. The earliest mention of this comes from the 12th century, so it may not be from Cuthbert's own time, but burial grounds are among the oldest Christian sites in Scotland and this one, like Ednam, is easily accessible by boat. The Slitrig burn joins the Teviot in Hawick town centre and anyone exploring the area by river would quickly come to the site of the old church. When St Cuthbert's Episcopal Church was built in the middle of the 19th century, it was deliberately placed as close to the old church as possible. Together with Drumlanrig St Cuthbert's primary school, it continues the Cuthbert association in that part of the town today.[6]

The story of the boy and the eagle (181) tells how an eagle brought food to them in an unexpected way. Always ready to teach from experience, Cuthbert turns this into an example of the 'kingdom of God'/God's way for the world, for a child who is travelling with him. Perhaps life had been unkind to this little boy. He does not expect any sort of kindness from strangers and does not think to share much with others himself. Cuthbert introduces him to a new experience. If this story has a historical basis, the eagle may have been a white-tailed sea eagle or an osprey. Both were present in this area as late as the 19th century but they were driven to extinction, mainly because they were seen as being in competition with anglers. Today, there are ospreys in the Borders once more, but they are still endangered and you'll be very lucky to see one.

Cessford Castle

The Border countryside is dotted with Pele towers, fortified houses where people took refuge from their enemies in time of war. From a distance, Cessford Castle looks like just another one of these, but once you get within a field's breadth of it, you begin to get a sense of the power which once emanated from this crumbling mass, riven with cracks from top to bottom, but still dominating the landscape. The Kers who lived here were often Wardens of the Middle March, responsible to the king for the peace of the area. It was a rough kind of peace, however, and the names Ker and Kerr (originally the same family) figure largely in stories of the Border

A huge crack rends the massive wall of Cessford Castle near Morebattle

reivers.[7] There was a prison in the castle and it was a fortunate man or woman who approached as a friend rather than an enemy. From the top of the ridge behind the tower, you can still see one of the great fireplaces at the top of the house. Here the laird and his family would entertain while prisoners languished in the dungeon below. The ruins are extremely unsafe today and should not be approached.

In August 1581, during the wardenship of William Ker, a traveller stayed overnight here and said something which could have cost him his life. The event was later described in a letter by the traveller himself and is a perfect example of how not to have a quiet conversation about religion:

> As soon as I arrived in Scotland, I was obliged to repair to the residence of the Warden, a Calvinist, who resides at a place called Cessford... After supper they held what they called a chapter. One of the ministers, for there were three present, read a Psalm, another delivered a short address, during which the Warden and his wife, and many gentlemen of noble birth and high position who were also present, listened reverently with heads uncovered.

The traveller did not take off his hat. When challenged to show reverence for the Word of God, he replied that 'Scripture wrongly expounded is not the Word of God'. He was a Catholic priest on his way to Edinburgh to see the king. His name was William Watts. It's hard to know whether to be appalled by his narrow-mindedness or amazed by his courage. Just a few miles away, over the border in England, Catholics faced the death penalty. Indeed, that was part of the reason for his visit. He hoped to persuade the young King James VI to provide a safe haven for English Catholics fleeing across the border, to tolerate Catholics in his own country and maybe even to become one himself. Watts also needed to know how hostile or friendly people like Ker might be. This is probably why he took the dangerous step of revealing his own identity. His beliefs about the Bible are intolerant by modern standards, but he was living in intolerant times and it's a tribute to all present that the 'hot controversy' which followed was fought with words and ideas only. In the end, Ker seems to have been impressed by Watts. Perhaps he admired his boldness. He said he would be less quick to condemn 'papists' in future and gave him a safe-conduct for the rest of his journey.[8]

Morebattle

Morebattle was once an outpost of Lindisfarne. In 670, when St Cuthbert was in his mid-thirties, King Oswy of Northumbria gave the monks of Lindisfarne a gift of land here.[9] We do not know whether Cuthbert had anything to do with this, but he would have known about it. If he had not visited already, he almost certainly did after he was made bishop, since he made a point of visiting people in far-flung parts of his diocese.[10] It used to be said that the Cuddy burn near Linton (p.104) was named after him but 'cuddy' has other meanings as we have seen.[11] Morebattle was a lochside settlement in those days (the name comes from the Old English *mere* and *botl*: 'the building by the lake') and the first church was probably in the area now known as Heughhead, near the present-day Church of Scotland.

Morebattle church

There have been at least three churches there: the Anglo-Saxon one, a later one administered from Glasgow Cathedral and the existing one, built in 1757. Some, possibly all, of these churches were dedicated to St Lawrence and 'Lowrie's well' below the churchyard, is named after the same saint. This was a public water supply till last century and was used far and wide for baptising babies.[12] No one seems to know when Lowrie, alias Lawrence, became Morebattle's patron saint but St Lawrence the deacon was certainly known in Northumbria in Cuthbert's day. Soon after the Synod of Whitby, the Pope sent a relic of St Lawrence to King Oswy as a present and there was a chapel of St Lawrence in Wearmouth, near present-day Newcastle.[13] In the Irish tradition, churches were usually named after the founder of the monastic 'family' to which they belonged, Columba for example. By honouring Lawrence, the Northumbrian Church showed its new orientation towards Rome, but it also honoured someone who cared more for people than for power and wealth. St Lawrence was, in effect, the Vatican treasurer of his day. He was put to death in third-century Rome for refusing to hand over the Church's money to the emperor. Faced with the equivalent of a police raid, he quickly gave the money away to the poor and paid for it with his life.

The murals inside Morebattle church are by the artist Jane Cowan, daughter of Thomas Leishman (p.105), who lived nearby and favoured such 'high church' activities as the saying of the Creed and the Lord's Prayer. Since the time of the Covenanters, Presbyterians had tended to associate these with forms of worship imposed by kings and bishops, though in fact they had been part of the original Reformed liturgy of John Knox.[14] In 1692, one Kelso preacher is said to have described the Lord's Prayer and the Ten Commandments as 'old rotten wheelbarrows to carry souls to hell'.[15] This was an extreme view but many Presbyterians preferred prayers composed by the minister, either beforehand or extempore. Jane Cowan's murals represent a change of attitude. There are also three stained-glass windows in the church: the women at the empty tomb, the Emmaus story (p.200) and the parable of the sower, placed in such a way that the minister could see it as he went up into the pulpit to 'sow the Word of God'.

Morebattle church. Limited parking on street, unreserved; heavy iron gate at entrance to churchyard; no steps; wide level path with hard surface; approx. 70 yds from gate to church; shallow ramp at church door; pews; public toilets in main street opposite Post Office.

Morebattle churchyard

At the beginning of the 18th century, Morebattle churchyard would be full once a year in June, from Friday to Monday, for the 'communion season'. This was the normal way of celebrating communion in the Church of Scotland at the time, and it drew crowds and visiting ministers from a wide area. Thomas Boston, later a famous diarist and minister of Ettrick, was a regular visitor in the early

1700s, though he left early one year, upset at only being allowed to preach once.[16] The usual pattern was for Friday to be a fast day with two sermons; two more sermons were preached on Saturday while the elders and ministers were examining people about whether they were morally fit to take part or not. On Sunday, there might be another sermon;1 then came the solemn moment, 'the Lord's Supper' itself, followed by a thanksgiving service on the Monday with two more sermons. Canopies were set up in the churchyard to protect preachers from the weather and in some places the communion itself was served outside. People sat at long tables covered with white linen and some cried out with emotion as they received the bread and wine.[17]

Communions were extremely popular. Indeed, in some places, employers complained that too many working days were lost through people gallivanting off to 'Holy Fairs' as they were called.[18] Not everyone's attention was always fully taken up with spiritual matters. Like the holy days of an earlier age, these were great social occasions and maybe God was also present among the picnic baskets. Certainly, communions provided a great opportunity for meetings between old friends and old enemies, lovers and strangers. Robert Burns had his own irreverent perspective on the matter:

> 'There's some are fou o'love divine;   (full/drunk)
> There's some are fou o'brandy
> An' minie jobs that day begin
> May end in houghmagandie   (hanky panky/sexual activity)
> Some ither day.[19]

There was a different mood in the churchyard in March 1725. The crowd was hostile and excited. Men were prising the lead off the windows of the old church and climbing in. Other men with collie-dogs were guarding the door. A new minister, Mr Christie, was to be ordained that morning, but he was not the people's choice. He had been chosen by the heritor, the Duke of Roxburgh, as was normal in Scotland at that time, but 'patronage' – the system of allowing local landowners to appoint ministers – was becoming increasingly unpopular. Christie arrived, accompanied by his supporters. Unable to enter the church, they tried to hold the service outside, but a scuffle broke out and soon cudgels were flying and women were hurling divots. The ordination party withdrew and Christie was ordained in Linton, the neighbouring parish.[20]

All this was part of an argument which had dogged Scottish church life since the Reformation and would continue into the early 20th century. It surfaced in many forms but centred around the question of authority. Who was in charge? Who was qualified to interpret the will of God and carry it out: the king, the bishops, the local landowner, local clergy and elders or even just ordinary people inspired by the Holy Spirit? There had been tussles like this before between popes and kings, but now the debate was taking place within one small country, with more and more voices crying to be heard.

Extracts from Morebattle church accounts, 1726–34.[21]

For 2 trees from Berwick for a bridge	*£3:12s*
To the glazier for mending the kirk windows	*£2:00s*
To a poor old man	*£0:01s*
To a mother that had 9 children at 3 births	*£0.06s*
To 5 persons distressed by the Turks	*£0:06s*
For a load of coals for Jean Hall	*£0:16s*
For cheese, tobacco and pipes for Jean Hall's funeral	*£3:14s:3d*
To the stranger poor at the Sacrament	*£1:17s*
For precenting in the kirkyard at the Sacrament	*£0:12s*
To William Bennet for setting up the tent & other work	*£5:00s*
For 11 yards of linen to be a communion table cloth	*£8:05s*

At some point during your stay, stop at the gate opposite the Temple Hall Hotel and look across to Linton. This tiny hamlet once had its own green and cross. The church on its grassy mound is a little gem, so you might like to make a detour to see it. Bear in mind, however, that if you are walking towards Yetholm, the next stage of St Cuthbert's Way is steep and demanding. If you do decide to go, leave Morebattle on the Yetholm road and instead of turning right towards Hownam, turn left, then left again towards

Kelso. Cross the bridge and continue for about three quarters of a mile till you reach a lodge-house on the left and a lane leading down in front of it. The church is at the bottom of the lane.

Memorial stone in the wall of Linton kirk

Linton

Facing outwards from the door of Linton church, you can see exactly where Morebattle loch used to be. The fields between here and the village are still liable to flooding. The tympanum above the church door is unique in Scotland and badly weathered but you can still make out a rider on a galloping horse bearing down on some kind of creature. Recent opinion explains this as a Norman knight killing two bears,[22] but in local legend it commemorates the slaying of the 'Linton worm'. This ferocious winged creature with poisonous fiery breath is said to have lived in the hills nearby. It frightened people so much that they were afraid to go either to market or to church because of it, till a Norman knight, William de Somerville, killed it by putting a burning peat on the end of his lance and sticking it down the creature's throat. He received the Barony of Linton as a reward and was made king's falconer.[23] The blip on his arm is said to be a falcon. Somerville did in fact became Baron of Linton in 1160, at around the same time as the church was built, so it's possible that he is indeed the rider, but what is he doing and why does this particular scene stand over the doorway of his local church? Did he simply like hunting scenes? Or did he cast himself as a figure in an older myth: St Michael and the devil perhaps, or St George and the dragon? There are other myths like this in the Anglo-Saxon tradition: Thor's battle with the world serpent, Woden's combat with the 'worm' and Beowulf's battle with Grendel 'the grim demon... who inhabited the fastnesses of moors and fens'.[24] Perhaps William wanted his new tenants to know that he was at least as good as any Anglo-Saxon hero.

A local history describes some of the ministers who have served here since the Reformation.[25] In the 17th century, the unpopular absentee John Balfour let the place go to rack and ruin, tried to suppress a local Pasche play and eventually resigned having contracted 'ane illicit and unhallowed marriage'.[26] He was followed by Robert Ker, the first regular parish minister, and Robert Boyd, the moderate Covenanter. In the 18th century, James Turnbull made 'endless journeys' on horseback to London to lobby against Window Tax. Houses were being taxed according to how many windows they had, leading landlords and low-income families to block up their windows, with disastrous results for public health. Turnbull wanted his poorest parishioners to be exempt. Andrew Ogilvie was remembered as 'a little old man mounted on a grey horse' picking his way across Graden Moor to christen a sick child.

Thomas Leishman and his son James were Linton ministers one after the other from 1855 till 1935. Both worked at reclaiming earlier traditions of the Reformed Church, particularly in the field of worship and inter-church relations. Their ideas seem so normal today that it's hard to believe they were once controversial.[27] In

1904, just before he retired, Thomas Leishman held an open-air service on Christmas Day, by the ruins of Hoselaw chapel a few miles away.[28] Christmas was not a holiday in those days so the thirty or forty farm workers who turned up for it wore their ordinary clothes and went straight back to work afterwards. 'I never thought I'd see the day,' said Leishman.[29] Christmas had not been celebrated in Linton for centuries. The Leishmans came originally from Govan and had many links with that other great Presbyterian dynasty, the McLeods.[30] Some of their ideals were carried forward in the work of George McLeod, founder of the Iona Community. I can't leave Linton ministers without mentioning the recently-retired Joe Brown who discomfited some of his parishioners a few years ago by turning up at a garden party disguised as a tramp. St James taught that Christians should welcome rich and poor alike to their gatherings (James 2.1–5) but my lips are sealed about what happened to Joe Brown.

The tiny 'Nunc dimittis' window to the right of the communion table is by Douglas Strachan (1875–1950), one of the leading stained-glass artists of his day. Strachan worked with Robert Lorimer on the National War Memorial in Edinburgh Castle and also made a window for the Thistle Chapel in St Giles Cathedral. The Linton window shows Simeon recognising the baby Jesus as 'a light to the nations' with Mary and Joseph looking on. Mary is carrying a basket of pigeons, the offering traditionally made by poor women on the birth of their first son.[31]

The Norman font was found in a nearby smiddy where it was being used for cooling the irons. It's big enough to immerse an entire baby, as was the custom in medieval times. There's a tradition that in the days of the Border reivers, the right hands of baby boys would be held out of the water during baptism so that in later life they could wield a broadsword without risk of mortal sin.[32] The story may be apocryphal, but it highlights the problems of growing up in a culture of violence in any age.

Notes

1   Royal Commission for Ancient and Historical Monuments, *Roxburghshire*, vol.1, 124; vol.2, 487. Charles Alexander Strang, *Borders and Berwick: an illustrated architectural guide*, Edinburgh, 1994, 121.

2   Correspondence of Sir Robert Kerr, First Earl of Ancrum and his son William, Third Earl of Lothian, ed. David Laing, Edinburgh, 1875. Vol. II, 488

3   op. cit. Vol. I.108–125.

4   op.cit. Vol. I. cl.

5   *History of the Berwickshire Naturalists Club*, 21, 1909–13, 221–1. Cormac Bourke, 'The handbells of the early Scottish church', *Proceedings of the Society of Antiquaries of Scotland* 113, 1983, 464–8. At the time of writing the bell is in store in the museums department in Duns.

6   The earliest record of the medieval chapel comes from Reginald of Durham who says that it was an outlying chapel of the church at Cavers. This need not mean that Cavers was an older church: cf. Melrose Abbey which had an outlying chapel of St Cuthbert at Old Melrose. J. Raine, *St Cuthbert*, Durham, 1828, 44; *History of the Berwickshire Naturalists Club* 14, 143–4.

7   The Kers of Cessford and the Kerrs of Monteviot were distant cousins, the 'r' spelling both relationship and rivalry.

8   According to James Fleming Leishman, this was Robert Persons (recte Parsons) S.J., travelling under the alias Mr Redman. It's more likely, however, to have been Parsons' envoy, William Watts. Leishman, *Linton Leaves*, Edinburgh, 1937, 47; cf. Thomas McCoog, *The Society of Jesus in Ireland, Scotland and England 1541–88*, Leiden, 1996, 178.

9   *History of Morebattle and District*, Scottish Women's Rural Institute, 1966, 5.

10 Bede, *Life*, 29–33.

11 Leishman, *Linton Leaves*, 21. Cf. the Cuddy fields in St Boswells.

12 *History of Morebattle and District*, 22.

13 Bede, *EH,* 3.29. The date 655 given in the Penguin edition seems to be a misprint for 665. Plummer suggests 667. *Venerabilis Bedae Opera*, xx (Wighard's visit to Rome).

14 J.H.S. Burleigh, *A Church History of Scotland*, Edinburgh, 1983, 188–257.

15 John Dickson at Kelso Meeting House, 1692. Quoted in James Fleming Leishman, *Linton Leaves*, Edinburgh, 1937, 58.

16 Thomas Boston, *A General Account of my Life*, ed. George D. Low, Edinburgh, 1908, 141–2; *Memoirs*, 241.

17 Boston, *A General Account,* 142, 195.

18 Callum G. Brown, *Religion and Society in Scotland since 1707*, Edinburgh, 1997, 73.

19 'The Holy Fair', *Complete Poems and Songs of Robert Burns*, Glasgow 1995, 31–7.

20 J. Tait, *Two Centuries of Border Church Life*, Kelso, 1889, 44–55.

21 Tait, op.cit. 60–64

22 Strang, *Borders and Berwick*, 120.

23 *History of Morebattle and District*, SWRI, 1966, 7.

24 *Beowulf* 2, ed. David Wright, Harmondsworth, 1970, 29. On Woden and Thor, see Henry Mayr-Harting, *The Coming of Christianity to Anglo-Saxon England*, 3rd edition, London, 1991, 26–30. A tenth-century stone cross slab from Isle of Man shows Woden with a raven on his shoulder, fending off a wolf with a spiked

implement. There is something (his leg?) in the wolf's mouth. Claire Stancliffe, *St Oswald: Northumbrian King and European Saint*, Stamford, 1995, plate 24.

25 *Linton Leaves*, 50–8, 84–6, 90–8.

26 The Pasche play included characters such as Robin Hood, Little John and the Abbot of Unreason. The players were admonished by Kelso Presbytery and excommunicated for 'open contempt and abuse of the Sabbath.' The tradition continued, however, into the 20th century. *Linton Leaves*, 51.

27 *Linton Leaves*, 139, 181.

28 The chapel was rebuilt in 1906.

29 *Linton Leaves*, 172.

30 Matthew Leishman of Govan (Thomas's father) and Norman McLeod 'of the Barony' were both leaders of the Middle party at the Disruption. *LL*, 103; *DSCHT* 479; Thomas and James Leishman and John McLeod of Duns (later of Govan) were all leading members of the Scottish Church Society. *LL*, 99, 135 and *DSCHT*, p.756 and Thomas Leishman gave the John McLeod memorial lecture in Govan in 1904. *Linton Leaves*, 174.

31 The story is told in Lk.2.22–35.

32 *Linton Leaves*, 28.

Accidental 'sculptures' of animals' heads on a rock outcrop on Crookedshaws Hill above the Bowmont Valley, between Morebattle and Yetholm

Morebattle to Yetholm

Kale Valley

The road climbs steeply out of Morebattle, then drops down into the Kale Valley and joins the Hownam road. St Cuthbert's Way turns left soon afterwards, over a little bridge. Here, you are near the site of a 'blanket preaching' which takes place every fifty years at Gateshaw Braes a little further up the road.[1] This open-air service commemorates the first ordination to the Secessionist church in 1739 – not just the first in the Borders, but the first in Scotland.[2] John Hunter, who was ordained that day, had been an assistant teacher in Linton school. We do not know if he was present at the affray in Morebattle churchyard 14 years earlier. He would certainly have heard of it. Since then, four Church of Scotland ministers had left the Kirk over the issue of patronage and set up on their own. Hunter was the first new minister to be ordained by them. His 'parish' was enormous, stretching from Morebattle, Stichill and Ashkirk to parts of East Lothian, Berwickshire and Northumberland. They had no church buildings of their own and it says a lot for the fervour of this little flock that they held their services outside, even in the depths of winter. In January 1740, just three months after his ordination, Hunter caught a chill and died; but the movement which he represented is still remembered today.

Memories of the Covenanters were still very much alive in the area at the time. In 1684, James Muir of Cessford and John Gilry and John Kerr, both of Hownam, had been executed in Edinburgh for their part in the uprising of 1679.[3] In the same year, a former minister of Linton, Robert Boyd, had been imprisoned in Edinburgh for his Covenanting views. Times had changed since William Kerr was a Covenanter in the 1640s. (p.95) Most landowners were now firmly back in the royalist fold. The execution of Charles I had shocked most people in Scotland and when the monarchy was restored in 1660, the authorities moved against those who persisted in not accepting state control of religion.[4] Boyd was one of hundreds of ministers who lost their parishes over the issue in 1662.[5] In many cases, their congregations followed them and illegal open-air services or 'conventicles' were held in out-of-the-way places, including one on the banks of the Kale below Morebattle church.[6] As the persecution grew, so resistance hardened, culminating in armed confrontation and the defeat of the Covenanters at Bothwell Bridge in 1679. It was in the aftermath of this that Muir, Kerr and Gilroy lost their lives.

The Secessionists saw themselves as continuing the Covenanters' struggle for religious freedom. Not everyone shared this opinion. Hunter, for example, had applied to the established church and been turned down for the narrowness of his views.[7] If Presbyterians remember and celebrate him today, this is largely because patronage was eventually abolished in the Kirk and groups like the Secessionists came to be seen as pioneers rather than trouble-makers. Most of the original splinter-groups have since been reunited, and the last time there was a 'blanket preaching' at Gateshaw, in July 1989, the mood was one of reconciliation.

Wideopen Hill

All over the world, there is a tradition of holy mountains: the Temple Mount in Jerusalem, K2, Mount Fuji, Uluru in Australia. Wideopen Hill is nowhere on this list and maybe that is a good thing. In John's Gospel, Jesus has a conversation with a woman about traditional sacred places: they are sitting beside a holy well near a holy mountain in Samaria. Both the mountain and the well were associated with Jacob, their common ancestor; she assumes that Jesus, being a Jew, will think that the temple in Jerusalem is a holier place; he surprises her by saying that attitude is more important than place where God is concerned and that people who worship 'in Spirit and in truth' can turn to God wherever they are, regardless of tradition. That, he suggests, is the way of the future.

Primside Mill

Coming down from Wideopen Hill, you rejoin the Yetholm road at Primside Mill. This old mill on the Bowmont Water was home to Andrew Rutherford Blythe, great-nephew of Charles I Blythe, king of the Yetholm Gypsies. Andrew never took to Travelling himself. Instead, he became a teacher and was for many years Session Clerk of the parish church in Kirk Yetholm. He's remembered as having had a curiously rusty voice and an Ulster overcoat with one empty sleeve. He had lost an arm in a shooting accident as a boy. His teaching career began while he was living with a shepherd's family high up in the Cheviots. A school inspector passed by, saw that the children could read and write, and appointed Andrew to the school nearby where he taught for nearly fifty years. He returned to Yetholm in later life but never married. When he died in 1934, he left £3,000 to the church, to buy coal for old people in the village, and to Kelso Hospital. The chiming bell is another part of his legacy as are the windows behind the communion table.[8]

Town Yetholm and Kirk Yetholm

Town Yetholm and Kirk Yetholm are separate villages. St Cuthbert's Way runs between them along the banks of the Bowmont Water. There are no shops in Kirk Yetholm or between there and Wooler, so if you need supplies, be sure to get them in

Town Yetholm on the way past. The monks of Kelso had three acres of land in Yetholm with the right to build houses there for themselves, their workers and their animals. They also had a share of the common grazing and the right to 'pass freely across the brook which separated the two kingdoms'. This probably means the Shotton Burn rather than the Bowmont Water as they had land on the English side of the burn as well, with pasture for twenty oxen, twenty cows, five hundred ewes and two hundred other sheep.[9]

The haugh or meadowland between the two villages was, for centuries, the scene of a no-holds-barred ball game which was played every year on Fastern's E'en.[10] Before the Reformation, this was the Scottish equivalent of Shrove Tuesday, when people ate, drank and partied before starting the discipline of Lent next day. Fastern's E'en sports were still played on the haugh in the 19th century and celebrated afterwards in traditional style.[11] The bridge across the Bowmont was one of the first projects of the 'improving' minister, John Baird, from the parish church in Kirk Yetholm. Before that the haugh was often impassable and the two villages were cut off from each other.[12] He was also responsible for rebuilding the church. It used to be thatched, picturesque and damp. Now the hard black whinstone hides an unexpectedly cosy interior.

Baird was not the only minister in Yetholm at the time. At the end of the 18th century, most villagers left the parish church and built a Secessionist meeting house in Town Yetholm. Their first minister, Robert Shirra, is described as a lively, intelligent young man who did a lot of visiting in remote parts of the Cheviots, preparing his sermons out loud as he walked. In 1818, a church was built for a United Presbyterian group. Their minister, Peter Hume, started a Sunday school, the first in the area, helped to start a village library and had Yetholm connected to the Post Office.[13] It seems to have been a period for go-ahead ministers, outside the established church. When Baird arrived in 1829, he rose to the challenge. One of his most famous projects involved the Yetholm Gypsies. Yetholm folk nowadays sometimes weary of the Gypsy connection, but visitors remain fascinated by it, so I hope I may be forgiven for telling the story again at some length.

Short walk around Kirk Yetholm (0.7 miles) for those who can manage a few steps and one steep hill. Not suitable for wheelchairs. Can be muddy and exposed in winter. Starting from village green, unreserved parking, take main road towards Town Yetholm. Pass and/or visit church on right. Pavement on left avoids dangerous blind corner. Continue downhill as far as bridge. Look for St Cuthbert's Way marker on right. Ten steps down, with rail. Follow unsurfaced path along haugh. Slightly uneven. Follow waymarker through gate on right. Keeping Youth Hostel on your left, rejoin surfaced road. From there, about 150 yds of steep hill (no seats) brings you back to the village green. Nearest public toilets, including accessible one, in Town Yetholm, in lane approx. 100 yds west of hotel. Radar key.

Kirk Yetholm parish church. Limited unreserved parking at gate; wide gravel path; slight gradient; approx. 40 yds to church door; one step; pews.

The Yetholm Gypsies

An engraving published in 1882 shows a group of Travellers camping on the green at Kirk Yetholm, round a fire in front of a bow-tent. Behind them is the row of houses, once known as Tinkler Raw, now the High Street. 'Tinkler' originally meant 'tinsmith', a traditional trade of Gypsies and other Travellers.[14] Kirk Yetholm had a sizeable community of Travelling people and this is where most of them lived when they were not on the road. They were able to stay here as a result of a debt of honour, a Gypsy having saved the life of a local laird while they were both in the army.[15]

A visitor to Tinkler Raw in the 1830s was struck by the poverty of the younger families. Some of the older ones were more comfortably off, but others apparently chose to live simply: 'though possessed of some wealth [they] are satisfied with very poor accommodation... seeing it is part of their calling to profess

poverty'.[16] Betsy White describes similar ideas in her 20th-century
account of a Traveller childhood, *The Yellow on the Broom*: 'We
just lived one day at a time... travellers thought it a great sin to
hoard up things or money... and believed that the very planning
or hoarding would bring death or disaster to the person or project.
They were afraid too to be selfish – believing that anything they
were selfish with would bring bad luck.'[17]

Gypsy pilgrims

When Gypsies first arrived in Europe over nine centuries ago, they
often described themselves as pilgrims.[18] Some carried safe-con-
ducts from emperors, kings, even from the Pope, stating that they
were on pilgrimage and should not be molested. It's not clear
whether this was true or whether it was simply a survival strategy.
No records of such passports have been found in the Vatican library, but its archives are incomplete.[19] Like the Jews, Gypsies had
no country of their own and often got a hostile reception. They
described themselves as pilgrims to King James IV of Scotland and
in 1505 he signed a safe-conduct for 'Anthonius Gagino, Earl of
Little Egypt, to travel to Denmark'.[20]

From 1609, the mere suspicion of being a Gypsy in Scotland
was punishable by death.[21] Those who were not executed were
transported or survived by hiding their identity, not speaking their
own language in public, taking local surnames and living on their
wits.[22] The border provided a much-needed escape route in time
of trouble. It's difficult to separate fact from prejudice in non-
Gypsy accounts of how Gypsies lived. Outlaws by birth, they often
found themselves on the wrong side of the law and there are endless stories about Gypsy smugglers, poachers and thieves. No
doubt some of these are true, but minorities often get more than
their fair share of blame for crimes committed, as Baird recognised
at the time: 'True, such things are done,' he said, 'but I am not sure
that they do them, or that they are the only persons who do
them.'[23] By the 1830s, most Yetholm Gypsies supported themselves by making horn spoons, baskets and brooms which they
sold around the country, together with earthenware, needles and
thread, trinkets, rags, bones and scrap iron.[24]

Baird believed that travelling was the root of the Gypsy

'problem' and he set about trying to change them. His approach was high-handed and there are those who think he did more harm than good; but at the time people were surprised that he should feel any good will at all towards Gypsies and at least one gentleman lambasted him for being so soft and gullible.[25] Baird carried on regardless. He started a new parish school which Gypsy children and others were encouraged to attend. Often known as the Ragged School, it was one of the first of its kind in Scotland and was housed in the building which is now the Youth Hostel. He also started a boarding-out scheme so that Gypsy children could live with non-Gypsy families while their parents were on the road. This met with limited success, but the school fared better and by 1843 nearly all the Gypsy children were attending and doing well. Unfortunately, this was one of its best years. It was totally dependent on charity and struggled to survive in the decades that followed.[26]

The Bible Society agent George Borrow once wrote that Gypsies are 'quite indifferent to religious subjects' and that even when they appear to be religious, they are only so out of superstition.[27] The accuracy of his views can be judged from his similar – and wildly eccentric – opinion of Catholics and Buddhists.[28] Unfortunately, Borrow was regarded as the authority on the subject by William Baird, John Baird's brother, who uses Borrow to back up his own opinion that the Yetholm Gypsies had no religion. It's true that few of them went to church and that some were involved in nefarious activities, but most Gypsy groups do in fact have beliefs and a moral code of their own, and these are sometimes practised alongside Christian beliefs.[29] The Yetholm community may once have been the same; but in an age when tiny differences in doctrine could lead fellow-Presbyterians to fall out among themselves, it would not be surprising if the Gypsies kept their private beliefs to themselves and others failed to recognise, value or enquire after them. A few Gypsies in each generation did go to church and also to communion.[30] Others had their children baptised, sent them to Sunday School and sent for the minister when they were dying.[31] Interestingly, they followed the custom of medieval pilgrims in always setting out from the church at the start of each season on the road.[32]

One of them, Matthew Douglas, tried to join the church but gave up. He had been attending for some time when the minister, Mr Blackie, approached him about becoming a member. Douglas was keen and asked what to do next. 'Buy yourself a copy of the *Shorter Catechism*,' said Blackie. Douglas bought the catechism and studied it while he was out on the road. Six months later, he called at the manse. Blackie started questioning him on the Trinity, the Fall, the Sacraments and so on. Douglas sat 'dumb as an oyster' then suddenly got up, cursing 'thae carritches' (by which, presumably, he meant 'catechisms') and walked out. That was the end of that. His nephew, Tam Blythe, later became a Methodist class leader and Tam's father Charles I Blythe liked to boast that Tam could 'preach as well as Maister Blaikie'.[33] Charles himself could quote from the Bible as well as from Robert Burns and a later member of the Blythe family, Jocky, was beadle till 1944. I'm told that no local descendants of the Yetholm Gypsies are actively involved with the church today but elsewhere there are Gypsy Pentecostalists, Catholics, Baptists, Orthodox, even Muslims.[34]

Nowadays the only signs of Gypsy culture in Yetholm are photographs in pubs and cafes and the Romani names of the 'braw lad' and 'braw lass' who lead the annual festival: the *Barri Gadgi* and the *Barri Manashi*. By the end of the 19th century, most Yetholm Gypsies had either intermarried and settled down, emigrated or moved away. The enclosure of common land in the 18th century had made it more difficult to find campsites or grazing:

Ilka slap and bye-way steekit	(every gap, blocked up)
Field to field is patched and eikit	(enclosed)
And naething left for a puir body	
No, not a mouthfu' for the cuddy.[35]	(donkey/horse)

By 1875, new laws against vagrancy were making it harder still. Travellers still visit the Borders, especially for the St Boswells Fair (p.81) in June. Their right to travel is now recognised by law and local authorities are supposed to provide a certain number of camp sites for them. In the mid-1990s, however, Scottish Borders Council had the second-worst record in Scotland for meeting its target number of sites.[36]

Notes

1   A more frequent 'blanket preaching' takes place every year at St Mary's Kirkyard near St Mary's Loch.

2   Leishman, *Linton Leaves*, 82–3; 'Gateshaw Brae Celebrations' in *Kelso First United Presbyterian Church, Report for 1894*; Service sheet, Gateshaw Brae celebration, 2 July 1989.

3   Tait, *Two Centuries*, 46. 'Gateshaw braes celebrations' p.37. From Hownam, Tait mentions only Kerr, while the 'Gateshaw Braes Celebration' mentions only Gilry 'the wright'. Tait, ibid., also mentions a Henry Hall of Haughhead who was imprisoned in Cessford Castle.

4   Lynch, *Scotland*, 287–95.

5   It was in this same year that a violent confrontation took place in Ancrum over the settlement of an unpopular minister. The candidate allegedly beat a woman protestor with a stick and a group of boys threw stones at him. Some of the protestors, many of them members of the Turnbull family, were later fined or imprisoned. Four of the boys were scourged, branded and sold as slaves to Barbados. The woman's brothers were banished to Virginia and she herself was sentenced to be whipped through the streets of Jedburgh. Alexander Jeffrey, *An Historical and Descriptive Account of Roxburghshire*, Edinburgh, 1836, 267.

6   Tait, *Two Centuries*, 47.

7   Leishman, *Linton Leaves*, 82. *Kelso U.P. Church Report*, 40.

8   Donald Whyte, 'Rev. John Baird, 1799–1861', *Border Family History Journal*, 26, 1994, 5.

9   Tait, *Two Centuries*, 310.

10 W. Brockie, *The Gypsies of Yetholm*, Kelso, 1884, 135.

11 Anne Gordon, *Hearts upon the Highway*, Galashiels, 1980, 133.

12 W. Baird, *Memoir of the Rev. John Baird*, London, 1862, 10–12.

13 Tait, *Two Centuries*, 314–20.

14 It is unclear whether the Yetholm 'Gypsies' were more closely related to English Romanichal or to the Scottish Travelling people known as 'tinkers' by outsiders and Nachins/Nawkens among themselves. When George Borrow visited Queen Esther Faa Blythe in Kirk Yetholm in 1866, he estimated that she used about 300 Romani words and also some words of Irish or Gaelic Traveller cant. She was indignant about the latter. Gordon, *Hearts*, 100.

15 Alexander Jeffrey, *An Historical and Descriptive Account of Roxburghshire*, Edinburgh, 1836, 329. Another version of the story makes it a reward for recovering a stolen horse. R. Murray, *The Gypsies of the Border*, Galashiels, 1875, 15.

16 John Baird, *The Scottish Gypsy's Advocate*, Edinburgh, 1839, 13–14

17 Betsy White, *The Yellow on the Broom*, London, 1992, 130–2. First published 1972.

18 Angus Fraser, *The Gypsies*, second edition, Oxford, 1995, 60–83.

19 Angus Fraser, op. cit. 60–78. 111–2;

20 Fraser, ibid.

21 The Act Anent Gypsies, 1609, was the most severe of several legal measures taken against Gypsies in the reign of James VI. The relevant passage reads: 'It shall be lawful to condemn and execute the Gypsies to death, on proof made to this effect only, that they are called, known, repute and holden Egyptians.' Similar Acts were passed in 1616, 1619 and 1620. Some Scots ignored the law or offered the Gypsies protection. In 1615, for example, W. Auchterlonie of Cayrine

was pardoned for harbouring a group of Gypsies but in 1616 a Sheriff in Forfar was reprimanded for being slow to prosecute others. The law was put into effect. Several members of the Faa or Faw family were hanged between 1611 and 1636 and in November 1636 in Haddington several Gypsy men were hanged and the women drowned (or, if they were mothers, scourged and branded on the cheek) for the crime of being Gypsies. Joseph Lucas, *The Yetholm History of the Gypsies*, Kelso, 1882, 120–122.

22 Fraser, op. cit. 111–2, 136–142; Vic Tokely, 'The Kirk Yetholm Gypsies', part 1, *Border Family History Journal*, 31, 1996, 28.

23 W. Baird, *Memoir of the Rev. John Baird*, London, 1862, 66.

24 op.cit. 12.

25 Jeffrey, *Roxburghshire*, 335–7. W. Baird, *Memoir*, 66.

26 Gordon, *Hearts*, 50–2.

27 Quoted in Baird, *Memoir*, 17–18.

28 'Popery... is the oldest of the superstitions; and throughout Europe it assumes the name of Christianity; it existed and flourished amidst the Himalayan hills at least two thousand years before the real Christ was born in Bethlehem of Judea; in a word, it is Buddhism... ' *The Romany Rye*, London, 1903, 311. First published 1857.

29 Fraser, *The Gypsies*, 242–6. Cf. 237–42 though this deals with a particular group.

30 Gordon, *Hearts*, 30, 52; Brockie, *Gypsies of Yetholm*, 135; Adam Davidson, 'Present State of the Gipsies in Yetholm', 1862, in Baird, *Memoir*.

31 Baird, *Memoir*, 21; Gordon, *Hearts*, 30, 51; Baird, *Memoir*, 46–50.

32 Anne Gordon, *Hearts*, 33.

33 According to Charles I Blythe, his father, the Gypsy king. Brockie, *Gypsies of Yetholm*, 136, 134.

34 Fraser, *The Gypsies*, 312–16; *DSCHT*, 827–8.

35 Anon. Quoted in William Brockie, *The Gypsies of Yetholm*, Kelso, 1884, 134; Murray, *Gypsies*, 30.

36 The Secretary of State's Advisory Committee on Scotland's Travelling People, *Eighth Term Report 1995–1997*, 1998:49.

Kirk Yetholm to Wooler

Etheldreda's Chapel

St Etheldreda the Virgin used to be commemorated on the outskirts of Kirk Yetholm. This Anglian saint, also known as Audrey, was a contemporary of St Cuthbert. The Chapel of St Etheldreda has completely vanished today, but it was marked on maps until recently. Look left before you cross the Halter Burn and you can see roughly where it once stood: at the foot of the hill in front of you, where the burn crosses the English Border. Etheldreda married twice, lived with her second husband for twelve years and remained a virgin. If you find this difficult to believe, you're not alone. Even at the time, people were sceptical.[1] Bede tells us that she really wanted to be a nun and that her husband eventually gave up and accepted this. According to local legend, it took a miracle to convince him. The first time he agreed to let her leave, he changed his mind almost at once and pursued her as far as the convent at St Abb's Head. There, according to legend, the tide came in and surrounded her, finally convincing him that he had made a mistake.[2]

The historical version is slightly different. Etheldreda was an Anglian princess. Her first husband had died soon after they were married, so her father gave her instead to Ecfrith, king of Northumbria. There's no record of how Etheldreda felt about this but it was then, according to Bede, that she took a vow of perpetual virginity. After many years she persuaded Ecfrith that her true vocation was to the cloister, at first going no further than the convent on St Abb's Head (p.75) Later, she moved to Ely in Cambridgeshire and became an abbess herself.

Virginity was highly prized by many Christians at this time. St Patrick was delighted that so many of his Irish converts took vows of celibacy and Bede wrote a hymn in praise of virginity, honouring a long line of virgin saints including Etheldreda. The devil flees from her, he says: 'Zealous for evil, vanquished by a maid.'[3] Did Etheldreda really snub Ecfrith so completely? Perhaps she did, but if she was so keen to become a nun, why did she agree to be married, not just once but twice? Maybe she had no choice. Maybe her stubbornness was a protest at being passed around in dynastic marriages. However, there's another way of looking at all this. Ecfrith and Etheldreda had no children. According to the ecclesiastical marriage laws of the day, if she retired to a convent, the king was free to marry again. This is exactly what he did but, interestingly, he had no children by his second wife either.[4]

The Anglo-Saxon abbesses

Etheldreda was not unique. An unusual number of royal women became abbesses at this period, ruling over double monasteries of men and women. Iurminburg was Ecfrith's second wife. After his death, she received the veil from Cuthbert in Carlisle and also became an abbess. Ebba (p.75) of Coldingham was the sister of Oswald (p.31) and Oswy. It's not known whether she shared their exile among the Picts and Irish. Hilda, Abbess of Whitby, was a member of the same family. As far as we know, she never married and came to the religious life in her thirties with the encouragement of St Aidan. She emerges from the pages of the *Ecclesiastical History* as a person of natural authority, someone who gave equal value to study and to more immediate practical expressions of the faith: 'those under her direction were required to make a thorough study of the scriptures and occupy themselves in good works... '[5]

Cyniburh we know very little about, but like Etheldreda she was a former queen who went on to become an abbess. Ebba's niece, Aelfflaed, was dedicated to God by her father, King Oswy.[6] He vowed that if he won a certain battle he would dedicate his infant daughter to perpetual virginity. Thus, the course of Aelfflaed's life was decided for her when she was barely a year old.[7] Bede describes her as 'a sensible woman... well versed in the scriptures' and not inclined to stand on ceremony. She approaches Cuthbert with 'true feminine audacity' and on one occasion summons him to Coquet Island from his hermitage on Farne, to discuss the succession to the kingship with her. At the same time, she takes him to task for choosing to remain a hermit on his 'barren rock' when the king, her brother, wants him to be a bishop.[8]

How do we explain this crop of royal abbesses in the seventh century? No doubt the abbeys served a useful social function at a time when so many kings died young in battle, leaving capable energetic widows. The abbeys also provided a way of supporting the church while keeping land and wealth in the family. For some women, they were also a dignified alternative to marriage. Social arguments like these are shrewd enough in their way but it seems, from the religious writings of women at other periods, that such choices are not always, or even mainly, simply a matter of convenience or necessity. For some, the religious life was attractive for its own sake, a calling rather than a compromise.

Adders

Also at the Halter Burn parking area, check out the area between the two iron gates for adders. If it's a hot day, you may see them sunbathing around here, but they are very shy so you'll need to approach quietly. They won't do you any harm unless you frighten them. They are poisonous, however, so be sure to leave them plenty of time and space to get away.

Wild Goose Hill

Looking upstream from the wooden bridge, the hill with the long wavy ridge to the right of the white houses is Wild Goose Hill. In winter there are large numbers of wild geese in the area. Greylags spend the winter at Hoselaw on the other side of Yetholm and you may see them passing overhead here or grazing in the fields during the day. One of the most heart-stopping moments of autumn is the first babble of geese on a frosty morning or late at night as they wing their way in from Iceland by moonlight. Listen out for them between October and March. Here's a poem about them by the Borders poet Ian McFadyen:

> *ARRIVAL*
> *Nothing in nature moves me like the*
> *wild geese winging in, when in the*
> *cold October gloaming, the*
> *thin wash of sky is*
> *suddenly alive with*
> *high and shifting skeins like*
> *wide and raucous scaldic runes –*
> *from the edge of the Earth, a*

song that's nothing
elegant or mystical, but
raggedly, excitedly alive,
full of the eager, forward-straining
joy of pilgrim souls who
see at last before, below them the
green pastures, the quiet waters of
this their other, earthly, home. [9]

The Iona Community have adopted the wild goose as a symbol of the Holy Spirit. The intention is to remind us that, in the Jewish and Christian traditions, God's Spirit is not a domesticated thing to be managed by human beings. It comes and goes as it pleases.

Eccles Cairn on the ridge above Kirk Yetholm

Eccles Cairn
Just over the Border, Eccles Cairn lies off the path to the north. There are fine views from it, including a last glimpse of the Eildons. No one seems to know much about the cairn itself but the name 'Eccles' is often the only surviving clue to a very old Christian site. It comes from the word *eglés*, which is how the ancient Britons and the Picts heard the Latin *ecclesia*, church. Ecclefechan, Eaglesham and Gleneagles are all *eglés* names and Eaglescairnie in East Lothian is almost a direct equivalent of Eccles Cairn. *Eglés* is not always associated with a church building. It could mark a former gathering place or a piece of church property. Some *eglés* names may go back as far as the fifth century.

That's before the time of any known mission to this area, unless we include Whithorn.[10]

Cuthbert in the mountains

We have already heard how, as a young man, Cuthbert would deliberately seek out 'steep rugged places in the hills' where the people were so poor that other preachers dreaded to go there.[11] Dread is a strong word, but imagine setting out on a journey with no idea what you might find at the end of it: with no guarantee of a square meal, a comfortable bed or even a welcome. Some priests simply did not bother. There were parts of the country where people never saw a member of the clergy, let alone a bishop, from one year's end to the next.

Cuthbert was different. Maybe his own experiences of hardship and illness helped him. He knew what it was like to be cold, lonely and distressed. As a young man he had learned to fast and go without sleep; he had lived through the plague and lost Boisil, his mentor and friend. He had lived on Farne (p.143) and faced his own need and fragility. At the end of his life, in his two short years as bishop, he took to the road again. It was part of his job to celebrate the sacrament of confirmation, laying his hands on the heads of the recently baptised and tracing a cross on their foreheads as a sign of consecration by the Holy Spirit. A description of one of these occasions in a remote area between Hexham and Carlisle helps us to imagine what such gatherings might have been like on this side of the Cheviots: there was no church or any other kind of suitable building; people came together at a central point from all the villages round about and put up tents for Cuthbert and his companions. For themselves, they built temporary huts out of branches. Then, for two days, Cuthbert stayed with them, teaching and celebrating the sacrament.[12]

Some priests carried portable altars in situations like this and when Cuthbert's tomb was opened in 1104, a small silver altar was discovered next to his body. If this was his portable altar, as many people think, the silver covering was added later. The original was much simpler, made of wood, with five crosses on it, one in the centre and one at each corner representing the five wounds of Christ. It is truly pocket-sized, no bigger than a CD case, and can be seen today in the museum of Durham Cathedral.[13]

One of these gatherings was interrupted by a group of women carrying a young man on a stretcher. They laid him down at the edge of a wood and sent a message to Cuthbert asking him to bless him. This was not unusual. There are several other accounts of sick people being brought to Cuthbert while he was in the middle of doing something else. There's also an echo of the Gospel story in which a group of men bring a friend on a stretcher to Jesus for healing.[14] Bede wants us to understand that Cuthbert had become so closely identified with Jesus that he was able to perform the same kind of healing miracles. Many people nowadays have difficulty believing in miraculous physical healing, but can still appreciate the description of Cuthbert at work: he abandons the ceremonies, goes to where the young man is, sees how very sick he is, asks the crowd to move away. There's no showmanship here, just loving attention to another's needs.

Trowupburn

Lay brothers from Melrose worked all over the Cheviots as sheep farmers.[15] One of their granges or farmsteads was in the hills south of Elsdonburn at Trowupburn. Melrose Abbey was once one of the largest wool producers in Europe, famous for quality as well as quantity. Wool has long been a mainstay of the Borders economy. If you have woollen carpets at home, this may well be where some of them started out. Sheepfarming, spinning and weaving have put food in the mouths of local families for centuries. We have already seen how the linen-weavers of Bowden (p.70–71) had to adapt to the arrival of the great woollen mills. As these closed or went on short time, people turned their hands to other skills, electronics for example, although in recent times this has proved just as precarious. There is still a living to be scraped from sheep-farming but with fleeces fetching only about £2–3 each, the only profit nowadays is in lamb rather than in wool.

The College Valley

At Hethpool with its picturesque cottages, St Cuthbert's Way enters the College Valley. On the other side of the field opposite the cottages, it crosses the College Burn by a wooden bridge and turns left into a patch of conifers. This route can be very muddy even in dry weather. An alternative route turns left before the bridge, over a stile at the foot of the concrete ramp and follows the north side of the burn as far as the footbridge further down. You can hear the rushing of a waterfall as you approach. This is Hethpool Linn and there's a beautiful little gorge here overhung by trees. You can rejoin St Cuthbert's Way on the far side of the bridge or continue downstream to Kirknewton. At the time of writing, there are plans to provide hostel-type accommodation at Kirknewton village hall. Check with Wooler tourist information centre for details.

If you stay on St Cuthbert's Way, look out for hazelnuts in the woods beside the path. It's hard to resist picking them, but the squirrels need them more than we do. Hazels were one of the first bushes to reappear in the Borders after the last ice-age.[16] They have been around for about 9,000 years and still grow naturally in the College Valley. Ecologists point out the usefulness of places like these for their biodiversity and all that we can learn from them. I'm sure they're right, but what if we just love them, useful or not? Julian of Norwich, the 14th-century English mystic, had a vision once of a tiny object no bigger than a hazelnut, lying in the palm of her hand. What can it be, she thought, and the answer came to her: 'It is everything that is made.' She was amazed to think that something so small and fragile could survive at all but the answer came again: 'It lasts and always will last, because God loves it.'[17] The idea that God loves human beings is familiar, but Julian's view is broader: God loves everything that exists. To look on nature with a loving eye is to begin to see it as God sees it.[18]

Kirknewton

If you take the detour to Kirknewton, St Gregory's Church is worth a visit. It is named after Gregory the Great, the pope who sent Augustine of Canterbury to England in the sixth century to convert the Anglo-Saxons. There were British and Irish Christians in the country already, but Gregory seems to have ignored them. What's more, Augustine assumed a position of superiority which the Britons found arrogant and difficult to take.[19] Gregory must surely share a measure of the blame for this, but some of his ideas still take people by surprise. For example, he instructed Augustine to be flexible in his approach to worship, picking what seemed best from various sources and forming them into a new liturgy for the young church, rather than imposing a bland uniformity. He also allowed married clergy and placed great emphasis on pastoral care.[20] The monastic system was not really designed to meet the needs of people outside the monasteries, though in the Celtic world it often did – after a fashion. On the continent, the main official church network was the diocesan system. Each diocese or area was headed by a bishop who was supposed to provide pastoral care for all the people in his 'patch'. Some bishops neglected this side of their work and Gregory saw the need to remind them of it. He also taught that it was important to combine contemplation and action; and by action he meant practical material help. When Rome was suffering from famine, for example, we're told that he kept registers of people living below the poverty line and arranged regular distributions of food, including corn from the papal estates in Sicily.

Kirknewton church looks rather uninteresting from the north, but the south side is charming and parts of it are very old. Don't miss the stone carving of the 'Adoration of the Magi' on the left of the chancel arch. The kings or wise men of the Christmas story represent all kinds of foreigners and outsiders.[21] Some people think the ones at Kirknewton are depicted as Scots, but are those kilts they're wearing or knee-length tunics? The carving dates from around the 12th century and the walls in the chancel are immensely thick, built to withstand the Border warfare which reduced the church to rubble on more than one occasion.

Parking, unreserved. About 100 yds from gate to church door by level path. Gravel chips. One shallow step at entrance. Accessible toilet planned for the new village hall across the road. No information at present about keys.

Josephine Butler is buried in the churchyard at Kirknewton. Born at Millfield nearby, this daughter of a country squire shocked her contemporaries by taking up the cause of prostitutes. Sexually transmitted diseases were rife in the mid 19th century, particularly among soldiers. An estimated 25% of men were affected.[22] In 1866, a draconian law was passed to try to bring the epidemic under control. On the word of a single policeman, any woman merely suspected of being a prostitute could be forced to undergo a medical examination and detained for three months in hospital against her will. No witnesses were required and no measures taken against her supposed clients. Josephine saw the injustice of the law and campaigned to have it abolished.

To begin with she knew nothing about the sex industry. Her teachers were the street women themselves. She got to know them through working as a volunteer at the local workhouse, and quickly discovered that among the criminals and 'wild defiant types' there were single mothers, rape victims, the unemployed and the destitute. Their clients came from every class and profession. Working with an under-cover journalist and former brothel-keeper, she also uncovered a ghastly trade in children.[23]

Josephine had been brought up to believe in a loving and merciful God. On one occasion she told the street girls: 'a woman is always a beautiful thing. You have been dragged deep in the mud; but you are still women. God calls to you, as He did to Zion long ago, "Awake, awake! You, sitting in the dust, put on your beautiful garments."'[24] Prayer was an important part of Josephine's life. 'In Prayer, I am still, silent,' she wrote, 'waiting for the Spirit.'[25] She worked closely with Quakers, Baptists and the Salvation Army as well as with politicians and journalists. The law was finally repealed in 1883.

To rejoin St Cuthbert's Way, leave Kirknewton on the Wooler road and take the turning, right, to Old Yeavering. The field behind the cottages may be the site of a deserted medieval village. Once you are up past the cottages, look back along the Wooler road for the Gefrin memorial, a curved stone wall about 8 ft high. The royal palace of Gefrin (see below) was in the field behind it.

Yeavering Bell

If you stay on St Cuthbert's Way beyond Hethpool Linn, the path takes you towards Kirknewton Tors, also known as Torleehouse.

People passing here two thousand years ago would not have gone unobserved. There was an important iron-age hillfort on Yeavering Bell (the hill facing you, to the right of the wood) with stone ramparts 10ft thick. The main entrance was to the south, facing directly up the College Valley. Inside the rampart, there were some 130 huts and a second rampart enclosing the highest part of the hill. The cairn in the centre probably dated from the bronze age, older than the earthworks. No one knows exactly what happened on Yeavering Bell. The only water supply is a stream half way down the southern slope, so it's unlikely that large numbers of people lived there all year round. Bits of charred wood have been found on top, as well as flints, pieces of broken pottery, oak rings, quernstones and a mysterious jasper ball.[26] Archeologists suggest that a signal beacon might have been lit up there. It's certainly a good site for one. But if it was also once considered a holy mountain, people might have used it for prayer and worship as well.

Wild goats

The name Yeavering comes from the Brittonic words *gafr* and *bryn*, meaning goat hill. Look out for feral goats around here today:

> *The high mountains are for the wild goats*
> *and rocks are a refuge for the badgers.*[27]

The royal site at Gefrin

On the other side of Yeavering Bell, to the north, there was once a British royal site taken over by the Angles in the sixth century. This was the original Yeavering or Gefrin mentioned by Bede. There's nothing to see there nowadays except a monument and an empty field but people have lived in and around it since the late stone age. In Anglian times, there was a Great Hall here for the king, a temple and a stockade, probably for keeping the animals which were brought as tribute. Kings did not live here all the year round, but visited regularly to collect taxes, settle arguments and cement alliances. There was a wooden grandstand with tiered seats nearby and this was probably where the public business of the community took place.

Baptisms in the River Glen

One year, King Edwin brought a stranger with him, a tall dark man with a slight stoop, a striking presence.[28] His name was Paulinus and he was a Christian missionary. Bede says the people were excited and eager to be baptised, but they must have been apprehensive as well. A few years earlier Edwin had married a Christian princess from the south and now he had become a Christian himself. They must have wondered what this was going to mean for them. Paulinus stayed at Gefrin for over a month, teaching and baptising thousands of people in the River Glen nearby.[29]

It's true that people are sometimes converted unwillingly or in the heat of the moment, but in tribal societies, even today, people do sometimes convert in large numbers. There are also signs that the Anglians were no longer getting much satisfaction from their traditional beliefs. In another part of Edwin's kingdom, Coifi the chief priest declared that the old religion had never done him any good and that he had long suspected it was useless. Another man said that before listening to Paulinus, he had thought that life was like the flight of a sparrow through a banqueting hall on a winter's day: in one door and out the other, into the night.[30]

All this happened before Christianity came to Lindisfarne. The people baptised by Paulinus were probably the first Christians in the area. They must have been aghast at what happened next. In 633, Cadwalla the Briton led an uprising against Edwin and killed him. Cadwalla was a Christian but religion made no difference to him where enemies were concerned. He attacked the Anglians vigorously, Gefrin was burned to the ground and large numbers of people were killed. His fellow Britons probably saw him as a freedom fighter. Bede saw him as a ruthless barbarian.

Paulinus retreated to the south and never returned. Only when Cadwalla was defeated the following year did the Anglians begin to recover.[31] Gefrin was rebuilt, with a new church, but it remained vulnerable to attack and was finally abandoned in 685. It is likely that during this trauma some of the newly-baptised Christians turned to the old gods in desperation, just as they turned to them later (p.36) for help against the plague.[32] These are the kind of people Cuthbert and Aidan would have met during their pastoral visits.

Wooler Common

Wooler Common, on the outskirts of the town, includes an area which has been carefully thought out with disabled people in mind. Anyone who has ever been confined to a wheelchair knows how good it is to be able to experience hills and forests at first hand. At present, very few parts of St Cuthbert's Way are accessible to people with disabilities. This is particularly sad since pilgrimages traditionally included large numbers of people who were sick or unable to walk, travelling in litters or carts. Sometimes their friends carried them. There's an example from the 11th century of two paralysed people crossing the whole of France and Italy on the backs of donkeys.[33] Not exactly comfortable.

Wooler Common, then, comes as a pleasant surprise. It's still very new but will feel more natural after a couple of seasons. If you are a fit able-bodied person, you may not notice all the care that has gone into this rather special project, but look out for the little things which could easily be done elsewhere. Projects like these are more common in the USA, particularly in the National Parks. We are only just beginning here and have a lot to learn, but Wooler has made a start at least. The accessible area includes a nature trail (0.25 miles) along the forest edge, a little burn, a pond and picnic tables. There are longer walks nearby for people with working legs.

Path hard-packed gravel with passing places. Slope, level to moderate. No steps. Benches with backs at regular intervals. Handrail all the way round. Picnic tables. Parking unreserved but close. No toilets. Nearest accessible ones in Wooler High Street in bus station car park by the Black Bull. These are kept locked but can be opened with a Radar key. Bring your own or collect one from Wooler Tourist Information Centre across the road, open Mon–Sat.10am–5pm except lunch time (1pm–2pm) and 10am–2pm on Sundays, Easter to October. In winter, it may be possible to borrow a key from the Hill Folk Shop, 28 High Street, Wooler, open Mon.–Sat. 9am–5pm, closed some Thursdays and all day Sunday.

Wooler

Coming down into Wooler, you immediately get the feeling of having arrived in England. Perhaps it's just in the accents of the people. After all, the River Glen nearby is just a lower stretch of the Bowmont Water which you crossed just over the hill in Yetholm. Wooler is at the heart of Glendale and is an important market town. The Mart on the Berwick road is one of the busiest sheep markets in the country. In the 19th century, when fresh air was one of the few cures for tuberculosis, doctors would some-times send their patients to Wooler, if they could not afford to go to Switzerland. Among these patients was the young Grace Darling (p.142) who sadly did not recover. There have been churches on the site of St Mary's Church (near the market place) since the 12th century. At the bottom of Church Street on the right is a grassy mound with the large Celtic cross on top of it. The mound is known locally as the Tory and the cross is a 20th-century war memorial. In the days of Border warfare, there was a fortified tower here, said to be able to hold twenty horsemen. The Youth Hostel at the south end of Cheviot Street was built for the Land Girls during the Second World War. These were young women who took on agricultural work to make up for the shortage of male labour. It came as a surprise to some people that women could drive tractors. Later, the hostel was used to house Latvian refugees.

Notes

1   Bede, *EH*, 4.19.

2   Jeffrey, *Roxburghshire*, vol.3., 232.

3   Bede, *EH* 4.20.

4   Stephanie Hollis, *Anglo-Saxon Women and the Church*, Woodbridge, 1992, 46–79.

5   Bede, *EH* 4.23.

6   Bede, *EH* 3.34.

7   This was in AD 655.

8   Bede, *Life*, 24, 34 and Anon. 4.10.

9   Ian McFadyen, *Tom's Boat and other Poems*, Peebles, 1996. Printed by The Penycoe Press, 7 Bridge Street, Penicuik, Midlothian.

10 G.W.S. Barrow, 'The Childhood of Scottish Christianity', *Scottish Studies*, 1983, 1–15; Bede, *EH*, 3.4; Scholars disagree about the date of the Whithorn mission but few would now put it earlier than the middle of the fifth century. See Alan MacQuarrie, 'The Date of St Ninian's Mission: a reappraisal', *Records of the Scottish Church History Society* 23, 1987, 1–25; John MacQueen, *St Nynia*,

Edinburgh, 1990, 22–31; Daphne Brook, *Wild Men and Holy Places*, Edinburgh, 1994, 8–33.

11 Bede, *Life*, 9.

12 op.cit. 32. Anon.4.5.

13 Elizabeth Coatsworth, 'The Pectoral Cross and Portable Altar from the Tomb of St Cuthbert', in *CCC*, 287–301.

14 Bede, *Life*, 29, 30; Lk.5.17–26.

15 In later times many of the abbey's sheep-farms were let out to tenants. The number of lay brothers seems to have been seriously in decline by 1443. Dennison and Coleman, *Historic Melrose*, 26, 31.

16 Stratford Halliday, 'The Borders in prehistory', *BB*, 21.

17 Julian of Norwich, *Showings*, Edmund Colledge and James Walsh, New York, 1978, 130.

18 Sally McFague, *Super, Natural Christians: How We Should Love Nature*, London, 1997.

19 Bede, *EH* 2.2.

20 Bede, *EH* 1.27 Letter of Gregory to Augustine, questions 1 and 2. Meyr-Harting, *The Coming of Christianity*, 54–7.

21 Mtt.2.1–12; cf. Is.60.3.

22 E.M. Sigsworth and T.J.Wyke, 'A Study of Victorian Prostitution', in Martha Vicinus (ed.), *Suffer and Be Still: Women in the Victorian Age*, London, 1973, 221, f.67.

23 Nancy Boyd, *Josephine Butler, Octavia Hill and Florence Nightingale: Three Victorian Women Who Changed Their World*, London, 1982, 50–1.

24 Boyd, op.cit. 77.

25 Boyd, op.cit. 62.

26 Northumberland Archeology and Building Conservation Service, *Sites and Monuments Record report*, NT 92 NW 62.

27 Psalm 104.18

28 Bede, *EH* 2.16.

29 op. cit.2.14.

30 op.cit.2.13.

31 op.cit.2.20; 3.1.

32 Bede, *Life*, 9.

33 Pierre André Sigal, *Les Marcheurs de Dieu*, Paris, 1974, 34.

Cup and ring carving on a stone on Weetwood Moor above Wooler

Wooler to Fenwick

Before leaving Wooler, make sure you have enough food and water with you, as there are no commercial refreshment stops between Wooler and Beal crossroads. You might also like to check the tide-table for Holy Island on the door of Wooler Tourist Information Centre, and if you are interested in seeing the cup-and-ring marks on Weetwood Moor, the TIC may be able to supply directions for these. Beyond Wooler, St Cuthbert's Way runs through another area rich in prehistoric remains. Large numbers of cup-and-ring marks were carved onto the rocks of Weetwood/ Westwood Moor during the bronze age, up to four thousand years ago. No one knows exactly what these circular marks meant to the people who put them there. Some say they represent the sun, but this is only a guess. Cut into the living rock to last for ever, they may have had some religious significance, but circles can mean many things and the secret of these has been lost.

According to the Official Trail Guide, the nearest group on Weetwood Moor is just off St Cuthbert's Way to the south, a detour of just under a mile. They can be difficult to find but if you feel like having a go, try the following: once you are through the gate at the top of Weetwood Bank, follow the path ahead, bearing right. After 300 yards, St Cuthbert's Way forks to the left. At this point, 'take the right-hand track at the fork and follow this cairned track across the moor to a gate and stile and look for a cairn on the low outcrops to your left which indicates the position of the main group of rock carvings. There are more examples on other rocks in the vicinity. Return to St Cuthbert's Way by the same track.'[1] Another possibility is to make for the big antenna construction and search in rocks around there.

Coming down off the moor, cross the River Till at Weetwood Bridge. This old narrow bridge, closed to heavy traffic, was built in the 16th century and restored during the 18th, but people have been crossing the river at this point for much longer than that. In September 1513, the English armies crossed an earlier bridge here on their way to the battle of Flodden. They marched under the banner of St Cuthbert, claiming him as an English national saint who would certainly want to see the Scots defeated. The Earl of Surrey had made a special journey to Durham to collect the banner which was basically a portable relic, a piece of linen taken from Cuthbert's tomb and mounted on a red velvet ground. It was believed to be the Corporax or cloth which Cuthbert used when celebrating the Eucharist and was first carried into battle against the Scots in 1346. Flodden was its last appearance.[2]

Perhaps the saint's body had lain so long in Durham that his years at Old Melrose and his love for the people of Tweeddale and Teviotdale were forgotten. This must surely have rankled with the Scots, but it has to be admitted that they had similar traditions themselves. Their ancestors had carried the relics of St Columba into battle, equally determined to have a saint on their side, and several eminent churchmen were on the battlefield at Flodden, praying for a Scottish victory.

If there are tears in heaven, Cuthbert must surely have shed them that day as 40,000 men from north and south of the Border laid into each other with guns and pikes. Casualties were so heavy that, as night fell, neither side was sure who had won. The English claim of 10,000 Scottish dead may be exaggerated, but it's safe to say that tens of thousands from both sides of the border were killed, including the Scottish King, James IV, and key members of the nobility. The Archbishop of St Andrews was among the dead, as were the Bishop of the Isles and two abbots.[3] Opinions differ as to how far local people were involved. Some may have been little more than bystanders, but in Selkirk, where the king's bodyguard was traditionally recruited, it's said that of the eighty men who went out to fight, only one returned. The great lowland lament, 'The Flowers of the Forest', was inspired by the Flodden tragedy and is played each year at the Selkirk Common Riding.[4]

> *I've heard them lilting at ilka ewe-milking*   (singing, each)
> *Lassies a-lilting before the dawn of day*
> *Now there's a moaning on ilka green loaning*   (pasture)
> *The flowers of the Forest are a' wede awae.*   (carried off)

Doddington Moor

Doddington Moor lies straight ahead after the bridge, though in summer it's mostly invisible because of the trees. The part of the moor known as Dod Law is dense with bronze age cup-and-ring marks. There are also many signs of bronze age and iron age settlement: forts, camps, earthworks, part of a stone circle. On lower ground, in a 'sandy knoll' above the River Till, the grave of a prehistoric man was discovered in 1867. Reports at the time described him as a small person in his mid to late twenties, lying on his side in a stone cist, facing west. He was wearing a stitched leather garment and had a food vessel beside him, a flint and a flint knife. These are now in the British Museum.[5]

Also on Doddington Moor is a small cave known as Cuddy's Cave. According to local legend, this is where Cuthbert kept his sheep when he was a shepherd boy. However, the anonymous Life says that his shepherding days were spent in the hills near the River Leader, which flows through Lauderdale and enters the Tweed just above Old Melrose.[6] This seems to rule out Cuddy's Cave as the place where he was a shepherd. However, there are other Cuthbert connections in the area: a 'Cuddy's well' which used to exist near the cave and the place-name Wrangham which some people think is the medieval Hruringaham where Cuthbert visited Kenswith, his foster-mother.[7] If he worked as a shepherd after leaving her care, it's possible that this is where she lived and where he was brought up. If so, he would have to have spent a lot of time on the road, since Bede tells us that Cuthbert visited her 'often' from the monastery.[8] He does not say which monastery, but the passage occurs in the part of the Life which relates mainly to Melrose.

Holy places are often historically suspect, but they can also be stage-sets for the imagination, places to get in touch with powerful stories from the past and attend to levels of experience which are easily crowded out in everyday life. When Bede wrote about Cuthbert the shepherd-boy, he does not seem to have been particularly interested in where this happened. What mattered to him was the image of the shepherd-boy with all of its biblical associations.

> *The Lord is my shepherd, I shall not want.*
> *He makes me lie down in green pastures*
> *He leads me beside still waters,*
> *He restores my soul*
> *He leads me in the right paths.*[9]

The shepherd here is a protective loving God, but in ancient Israel community leaders (sacred and what we now call 'secular') were also sometimes described as shepherds, tending the flock of Israel on God's behalf. King David was one of these, and the last and greatest, so it was believed, would be the Messiah.[10] When Jesus calls himself the 'good shepherd', in John's Gospel, he appeals directly to both of these traditions: we are being told, gently but shockingly (to his contemporaries), that Jesus of Nazareth was the Messiah and also the shepherd-God incarnate. The shepherd image is found again in Matthew and Luke's Gospels, where Jesus describes God's particular care for the 'lost sheep' and demonstrates it in his own life.[11]

Bede wants us to understand that Cuthbert was a shepherd

in the same tradition. This could be simply a convention, a way of saying that Cuthbert was like Jesus, or David, or any number of other shepherd-saints. But if it is also true historically, then Bede probably saw it as prophetic, a sign of Cuthbert's future calling as bishop. To this day, a bishop's crozier or staff is modelled on a shepherd's crook, to show that he or she is supposed to be a shepherd of souls.

The Devil's Causeway

After West Horton, St Cuthbert's Way runs for 300 yards along the 'Devil's Causeway'. This is a section of an old Roman road which used to run between Corbridge and Tweedmouth. A little further on, towards Lowick, it becomes quite dramatic, cutting through the fields in a straight line for about five miles. I don't know how it got its rather sinister name. Perhaps it reminded someone of the broad, straight road that the fairy queen sings about in the ballad of Thomas the Rhymer (p.67). Did somebody once see this road as a parable? Or did they just not like its relentless straightness?

The narrow gate and the rough little twisting path are both used as images for the road to life in the teachings of Jesus, the way to the 'kingdom of God'.[12] This is not an invitation to religious exclusiveness. On the contrary, all kinds of unexpected people will find their way there, he says, while others, who call him 'Lord, Lord' and think their religious credentials are impeccable, will not. There's a warning here to religious people not to be self-righteous and exclusive; and an encouragement to strangers and late-comers.[13]

The Northumbria Community

Crossing the next stream, you come within a mile of Hetton Hall/Nether Springs, home of the Northumbria Community. This mixed ecumenical community has been based here since 1992 and still has a very young experimental feel to it, though it includes people of all ages, married and single. Not all Community members live on the premises. Some have homes of their own at a little distance. Others live further afield. This gives the place a feeling of connection with the outside world. At the same time, it has a quiet, contemplative atmosphere, with its own liturgy four times a day and two tiny cells in the woods for private prayer. The old walled garden has been turned into a 'prayer garden' where they also grow some of their own food. The Community is very involved in the creative arts and runs a nation-wide storytelling project in partnership with the Bible Society. There are Orthodox icons in the chapel and works by Catholic and Protestant writers in the library. St Cuthbert's Cave (see below) is visible from the garden and guests often make a mini-pilgrimage there. There is a year-round programme of retreats, but passing visitors are also assured of a warm welcome and a cup of tea, and an overnight stay may be possible.

St Cuthbert's Cave

This is one of the high points of the pilgrimage for some people. Caves are among the oldest sacred places on earth. Our ancestors lived in them and painted picture-prayers on the walls. All over the world, caves have been used by prophets, hermits, penitents and fugitives. Services have been held in them in times of persecution and some are still places of Christian worship today. No wonder, then, that traditions about a local saint have grown up around this one. Look for the natural cross on one of the sandstone boulders opposite the cave's mouth, with a niche cut to the left of it 'such as might hold a lamp'.[14] When Cuthbert 'sailed away, privately and secretly' from Old Melrose, did he come to a place like this before being 'constrained' to go down to Lindisfarne?[15] It's not difficult to imagine him living and meditating here at some time in his life. Two centuries later, did a band of white-faced fugitives stumble in here one night, carrying his coffin?

Lindisfarne was one of the first abbeys in Britain to be attacked by Vikings. It survived the first raid in 793 but between 830 and 845 part of the community moved inland to Norham for safety, taking some of their treasures with them. It's unclear whether Cuthbert's body was among these or whether it remained on the island to the very end.[16] After the last raid in 875, it was taken from its shrine and for the next eight years was carried about the countryside by a bedraggled group of monks seeking a permanent home. At one time it was believed that the name 'St Cuthbert's' was given to every place where his body rested. In fact, no one knows exactly where they went. It's possible that they spent some time in the Whithorn area.[17] Many churches of St Cuthbert trace their origins to that journey and that may be how the St Cuthbert's Cave tradition grew up as well. In 883, the sad procession arrived in Chester-le-Street and Cuthbert's relics remained there till 995 when a 'little church of wands and branches' was built for them in Durham. There were fears that the shrine might be desecrated by the Normans as they swept north in the late 1060s, but they were more respectful or perhaps just more subtle than expected. They adopted Cuthbert, recognising him as a saint, and in 1093 work began on a magnificent new building to house his body – the present-day Durham Cathedral.

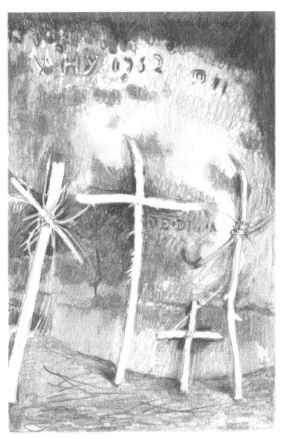

Graffiti and simple grass-tied crosses adorn the dark interior of St Cuthbert's Cave

Mons gaudium

In every pilgrimage there's a moment when you come over the brow of a hill or round a corner and, suddenly, your goal is in sight. Medieval writers called it the *mons gaudium*, 'hill of joy'. On a clear day, the *mons gaudium* of St Cuthbert's Way is the hill above St Cuthbert's Cave between Greensheen Hill and Cockenheugh. This is where you get your first glimpse of Lindisfarne or Holy Island, as it became known. It disappears again as you drop down into the next valley, but at the top of the crag opposite there is an even better view, if you don't mind a short detour. Go though the gate at the left-hand end of the crag, onto the track and turn right (St Cuthbert's Way turns left here). After about 50 yards, the view opens out before you and you can see Bamburgh, the Farne Islands and Inner Farne where Cuthbert and Aidan lived as hermits. Rejoin St Cuthbert's Way by the same path.

Aidan

Aidan is the neglected saint of this pilgrimage – undeservedly, since it was he who started the whole Lindisfarne tradition. He came here from Iona soon after Cadwalla's rebellion. The new king of Northumbria, Oswald, had been living in exile among the Irish, probably on Iona, and had been baptised there. On his return home, he sent to Iona for help in establishing a Christian kingdom. In due course, Aidan arrived with a small group of Iona monks. It can't have been easy for them. Aidan spoke so little English that Oswald had to interpret for him to begin with. He chose Lindisfarne to be his headquarters: an island like Iona, small and unpretentious with some good farm land; close, but not too close, to the castle at Bamburgh.[18]

Aidan was on good terms with his royal patrons but he liked to keep a little distance from affairs at court. He would come to banquets but leave early, accept gifts, then give them away.[19] There's a famous story about an extremely fine horse given to him by King Oswin. Soon afterwards, Aidan gave it away to a beggar, with all its royal trappings. The king was indignant. 'If I had known you were going to do that', he said, 'I'd have given you an old horse, not one of the best.' Aidan saw how attached the king was to wealth and influence; perhaps he struggled with that same attachment himself. 'What are you saying, your Majesty?' he replied. 'Is this child of a mare more valuable to you than this child of God?'[20] Bede tells us that Aidan never kept silent out of respect or fear but 'used his priestly authority to check the proud and powerful'. This seems to be an example of that fearlessness.

Aidan was interested in all kinds of people. When he was out walking, no one was above or beneath his attention. He stopped and spoke to everyone, whatever their rank or religion. If you had been walking here during the 640s you might have met him, padding towards you, greeting you in his Irish accent. He seems to have been quite direct, encouraging people to be baptised if they had not been, and strengthening others in their faith. It's interesting to see what Bede picks out as the essence of his teaching: 'live a good life and be generous to others'.[21] It was first and foremost a practical theology, a theology of goodness. At the same time, Aidan needed to be away from people sometimes to renew his acquaintance with the source of that goodness, and this seems to be why he went to Inner Farne, as Cuthbert did later, following his example.[22]

Bamburgh

Bamburgh was a royal seat. Its strong position on a rock, like Edinburgh Castle, made it an important fortress as well. People have held power and taken refuge on this rock since iron age times. Then, it was a Celtic site, occupied by Britons. The Anglians captured it in the 6th century and for a while it was their 'capital' north of the Tyne.[23] They lost it to the Vikings three centuries later. The wall round it was built by the Normans in the 12th century to keep out the Scots. The castle you see today is a Victorian restoration, but Cuthbert and Aidan would have been familiar with its rocky outline. Here, the Northumbrian kings held court and here their enemies came to attack them. Bede tells us how Aidan once saw smoke rising from the place as Penda of Mercia piled beams and wattles and thatched roofs against the walls of the castle and set fire to it, unsuccessfully. Aidan was on retreat on Inner Farne at the time, and we are told that, as he called to God for help, the wind changed direction and Bamburgh was saved.[24] Aidan had a church and a lodging near the town and this is where he died, leaning against a pillar by the wall of the church. King Oswald was eventually declared a saint too and pilgrims used to call at Bamburgh to visit his shrine in St Peter's Church.[25]

The Farne Islands

The scatter of islands off Bamburgh are famous nowadays for birds and seals. Boat trips run from Seahouses (April to September) and it's possible to land on Inner Farne and Staple Island where there is a large colony of puffins, terns and other birds. Before the light-houses were built, these islands were extremely dangerous to ship-ping. It's said that wreckers living along the coast would deliberately lure ships onto the rocks so that they could harvest their cargo from the shore. Holy Islanders were once suspected of praying for wrecks to happen.[26] By 1839, however, their intentions were clear and honourable: the men of the island built a lifeboat house and a boat, and a series of notice boards opposite the museum records the number of times they put to sea to rescue people in danger on the Farnes.

It was on the Farnes in September 1838 that the SS Forfarshire ran aground in a storm with over sixty people on board. Eight crewmen and a passenger escaped in a boat, leaving the rest to sink or swim. Twelve made it to Harker Rock where their cries reached the ears of William Darling, keeper of the Longstone Light. He set out in an open boat with his daughter Grace and, rowing through heavy seas, they made two journeys to the wreck and brought nine people to safety. Grace Darling became a national heroine overnight. It was considered an extraordinary thing for a young woman to do at the time, though it must have taken great courage from both of them.

Inner Farne is the largest of the inshore group, easily identi-fied by its lighthouse. In the 14th century, two chapels were built there by Benedictine monks from Durham: St Mary's and St Cuthbert's. Monks from Durham had been living there two at a time, plus servants, since 1255 and remained there more or less till the Reformation. They supported themselves by farming and col-lecting fish and seal-oil. They also had pasture on the mainland and received gifts in kind from local landowners. They ate well for the times: meat, fish and poultry, bread and butter, peas and beans. Their seasonings included saffron and mustard as well as salt and pepper. Newcastle Corporation gave them an annual allowance of wine and they brewed their own ale. They supplied food to the mother-house in Durham: one year, a porpoise for St Andrew's Day; another time, six dozen wildfowl and four puffins.[27] It has been described as a wealthy house but it was not exactly luxurious. Their asceticism was nothing like as fierce as that of Cuthbert or Aidan, but it was still more restrictive than most people would tolerate today.

It was Aidan who first used Inner Farne as a retreat. It's not clear how much time he actually spent there. Bede calls it 'his lonely hermitage' and says that he went there whenever he wanted to pray alone and undisturbed. Ten years earlier, however, he had written that Cuthbert was the first person brave enough to live there alone.[28] So either Bede changed his mind for some reason or Aidan had a companion, possibly a servant. Solitary prayer was very much part of the Irish tradition. Aidan's patron saint, Columba, used to go to the far side of Iona when he wanted to be alone for a few hours. For longer retreats he went to a neighbouring island, either on his own or with a few friends.[29] Other monks set off from Iona looking for a 'desert in the ocean' where they could live, possibly for ever, as hermits.[30] They were inspired partly by the Life of St Antony of Egypt who spent twenty years 'training himself in solitude' in the African desert. But behind that is the example of Jesus himself, fasting in the desert for forty days or slipping away into the hills to pray, late at night or early in the morning.

When Cuthbert came to Farne, things were difficult at first. Like the 20th-century hermit, Thomas Merton, he had longed for solitude for many years and was overjoyed when the abbot gave him permission to live alone.[31] But Cuthbert was not immediately at ease with the situation. Inner Farne was believed to be haunted and Bede says that he had to banish the demons before he could settle in.[32] Maybe he had anxieties about being left alone – and no wonder. He would experience cold and loneliness, cravings, loss of confidence. He would be taken far beyond his own limits, into that nowhere land where, as Lionel Blue says, you learn to see the

truth without illusion – beyond roles, beyond other people's opinions and beliefs.[33] Farne was always a 'battlefield' for Cuthbert,
though it was also his 'beloved hiding place' and he hated to leave
it, even when he was ill.[34] He did leave, reluctantly, when he was
made bishop and went back to visiting, teaching, healing and
being a shepherd of souls. He returned to Farne only to die and
would like to have been buried there but the community would
not allow it. After his death, pilgrims visited the island and were
shown the hermitage behind its rampart of earth, the guesthouse,
even the privy which he constructed out of driftwood.[35] Today's
visitors can see the remains of the two late-medieval chapels, the
outline of fields cleared and cultivated by the monks and a Pele
Tower which came to be used as a lighthouse. Little remains from
the time of Cuthbert and Aidan, except the island itself and the
stories.

Fasting

Cuthbert sometimes travelled without food, ready for whatever
came his way (p.181). If nothing turned up, he simply went without. He had been doing this for years and was used to it.
Nowadays, responsible walkers take emergency rations. Fasting is
one of those activities which many people find hard to understand
these days; how much more so those other forms of 'giving up'
practised on Lindisfarne and in Old Melrose: giving up warmth,
comfort, sleep, sex, washing, ordinary human company. Why did
they do it?

Exercises like these also appear in the early Irish Penitentials.
But penance was not the only reason for them. Celtic and Anglo-
Saxon warriors trained themselves in endurance, just as soldiers
and athletes do today. They learned to focus their energy and
ignore, temporarily, the panic-signals coming from their bodies.
Asceticism (from the Greek *ascesis*, meaning 'training') can be seen
as a kind of spiritual equivalent. It's not fashionable today, perhaps
because, in some churches, it has been over-used and misused.
However, in Cuthbert's day, the enemy was not food, sex, or one's
own body. It was selfishness. By practising non-attachment, even
to things which are good, the ascetics hoped to become less pre-
occupied with their own needs and more available to God and to

other people. It's an approach which can go disastrously wrong. Karen Armstrong, in *Through the Narrow Gate*, describes her own escape from it. But comfort can be a prison too – and a costly one.

Notes

1 Roger Smith and Ron Shaw, *St Cuthbert's Way: Official Trail Guide*, 46.

2 C.J. Stranks, *This Sumptuous Church*, 24.

3 Lynch, *Scotland*, 163.

4 Judy Steel, 'Border Traditions: the Common Ridings', in *BB*, 225–8.

5 Northumberland County Council Sites and Monuments Record Report no. NU 03 SW 12.

6 Anon. 1.5.

7 Colgrave, *Two Lives*, 324; Anon.2.7. But cf. Wrangholm near Old Melrose, p. 29.

8 Anon. ibid; Bede, *Life*, 3, 5, 14.

9 Ps.23.1–3; cf. Gen.49.24; Ps.80.1; Ezek.34.11–16; Is.40.11.

10 2 Sam.5.2; 1 Chron.11.2; Ps.78.70; Ezek.34.12; Mic.5.4..

11 Jn.10;1–16. Lk.15.3–7. Mtt.18.10–14.

12 Mtt.7.13; Lk.13.22–30.

13 Homily, Fr. John Creanor, Melrose, 1998.

14 M. Hope-Dodd (ed.) *Northumberland County History*, XIV, 1935, 130–1. A visitor in 1921 thought, from the condition of the tool marks, that the niche was not of any great age. *Berwickshire Naturalists Club*, 24, 276–8.

15 Anon. 3.1; Colgrave, *Two Lives*, 324; *HBNS* 24, 1919–22, 276–8. J.Raine thought he might have come here from Lindisfarne 'for purposes of seclusion'. *North Durham*, 1852, 215 Note.

16 The earliest sources differ on this point. *History of St Cuthbert* 9 and 20, in *Symeonis monachi Opera omnia/Complete works of Symeon the monk*, I.196–214., ed. T. Arnold, Rolls Series, London, 1882–5; I.G.Thomas, 'The Cult of Saints' Relics in Medieval England', unpublished Ph.D. thesis, University of London, 1974, 74.

17 Daphne Brook, *Wild Men and Holy Places*, Edinburgh, 1994, 62–5.

18 Bede, *EH* 3.3–5.

19 Bede, *EH* 3.5.

20 Bede, *EH* 3.14.

21 Bede, *EH* 3.5,17.

22 Bede, *EH* 3.16

23 Lady Armstrong, *Bamburgh Castle*, 1994, 2.

24 Bede, ibid.

25 Bede, *EH* 3.6.

26 Frank Graham, *Holy Island*, Rothbury, 1997, 14.

27 George Tate, 'The Farne Islands', *HBNC* III, 1850–6, 222–250.

28 Bede, *EH* 3.16; *Life*, 17.

29 Adomnán, *Life of St Columba*, 3.16–18.

30 Adomnán, op.cit. II.42.

31 Merton is perhaps best known for his autobiography *The Seven Story Mountain*, New York, 1948, but his journals, especially *The Sign of Jonas* (1953) and *Conjectures of a Guilty By-Stander* (1965) chart his journey from Cistercian community life to the hermitage which he finally entered in 1965. His other works include *The Wisdom of the Desert* (1960), *New Seeds of Contemplation* (1962), *The Way of Chuang Tzu* (1965), *Raids on the Unspeakable* (1966), *Zen and the Birds of Appetite* (1968) and his *Asian Journal*, published posthumously. He died in 1968.

32 Bede, *Life*, 17.

33 Lionel Blue, *My Affair with Christianity*, London, 1998, 94–5.

34 Bede, *Life*, 17, 22, 25, 37–9

35 op.cit. 18, 21.

Fenwick to Lindisfarne

Crossing the A1: Aeneas Sylvius

It's not often that a pope comes to England or Scotland but some time in the 1430s, the future Pope Pius II made his way from Berwick to Newcastle between the Kyloe hills and the sea. This is still a major route south. Between Fenwick and Lindisfarne, St Cuthbert's Way crosses the A1 and the main east-coast railway line. There were no special arrangements for this unusual visitor. In fact, he was trying to look inconspicuous. Aeneas Sylvius Piccolomini, as he was then called, was disguised as a merchant and was returning from a visit to the Scottish king, James I. It's not clear what this visit was about. Whatever it was, he was not keen to have to explain it to the English authorities.

He would have travelled home by sea had it not been for the near-shipwreck he had suffered a few weeks earlier on his way to Scotland. In fear of his life, he had vowed that if the ship landed safely, he would immediately go on a pilgrimage, barefoot, to the nearest shrine. The storm abated. Luckily for Aeneas, the nearest shrine was only about ten miles away at a place called *alba ecclesia*, possibly Whitekirk near Haddington. But it was the middle of winter and ten miles barefoot over frozen ground almost finished him off. He was so sick by the end that he had to be carried back to his lodgings on a stretcher.

He hated the short hours of daylight. He hated the Scottish climate. And as he walked down the high road to Newcastle, he was glad to think that he was returning to 'civilisation'. He was probably a bit bleary-eyed that morning as he hadn't had much sleep. Just outside Berwick, he had stopped for the night with a local farmer who entertained him into the wee small hours. Women from the houses round about came to stare at him as if he were 'an Indian or an Ethiopian'. Presuming that all Christians were pale northerners like themselves, they asked him if he had ever heard of the Christian religion. Aeneas took it all in good part. Then, at about two in the morning, his host suddenly got up to leave. He explained that he was going to spend the night in 'a distant keep' since the tide had gone out and the Scots might now attack at any moment.[1] He refused to take anyone with him: they would not hurt foreigners, he said, and the women would survive.

So Aeneas spent a memorable night with about a hundred women. If they were anything like their sisters north of the border, he must have felt a frisson of pleasure at the memory: (Scottish) women are 'comely and pleasing', he wrote, 'not distinguished for their chastity, giving their kisses more readily than Italian women (give) their hands.' The Berwick women sat round the fire 'cleansing hemp' and carrying on a lively conversation with him through an interpreter. There was a moment of panic when the farmyard dogs and geese sent up an alarm, but no Scots appeared and at daybreak Aeneas continued towards Newcastle reflecting that soon he would be out of 'this rugged wilderness, unvisited by the genial sun'.[2]

The tide table

There's a sense of excitement as you approach the sea. If everything has gone according to plan (p.24) you should know, even before you cross the brow of the hill, whether the tide is going to be in or out, but the open causeway is always a welcome sight: the gleam of wet sand and the island itself, like a mirage shimmering above the marram grasses. This is a place which still lives close to the great rhythms of nature. The causeway is a much-needed concession to the modern world but the islanders' lives are still ruled very much by water and the moon. At one time, everyone lived like this. Now, all kinds of technological advances have given most of us, in the cities of the developed world at least, the illusion that nature is under human control. No doubt it's more under control than it used to be, but every year people get caught by the tide at Lindisfarne and spend a cold few hours perched in the rescue box watching the rise and swirl of the sea and realising that they are not so omnipotent as they thought they were. Could this be one of the things which attracted Aidan to the island, this twice-daily lesson in humility? To avoid looking silly or worse, please check the tide table again before crossing. In particular, please note that the tide covers the pilgrim's way at least one hour before it reaches the causeway. So if you are taking this route, i.e. the route over the sands, be sure to allow yourself plenty of extra time. The currents can be extremely dangerous as the tide comes in. Do not attempt to cross unless you are sure it's safe.

Stones from the shoreline of Holy Island

Crossing the sands

I hardly ever cross to Holy Island without thinking of the story of the Israelites crossing the Red Sea.[3] It's a story which not everyone likes (all those dead Egyptians) but the Israelites were in a more desperate situation than most of us will ever know today. They were runaway slaves. They had been working for generations in intolerable conditions and had been subjected to a particularly brutal kind of population control.[4] It's a story which has powerful resonances for Jews today but others have found it speaking to them as well. When Paul Robeson sang:

Go down, Moses, way down in Egypt's land
Tell old Pharaoh to let my people go

he was understood all over the world, from the cottonfields of Alabama to the Welsh valleys and the Soviet Union. When the first followers of Jesus saw him taking on the oppressive forces of his own day, some of them expected him to lead a revolution and set up a godly state, there and then. In the months and years after his death, they were forced to think again. They came to believe that his message of good news to the poor was also good news to people enslaved by fear, cynicism, guilt or hatred. They became convinced that, in some way, Jesus was still with them, trusting them to continue where he left off, and that far from being swept away by the waters of death, both he and his message had emerged stronger than ever. Perhaps this is why the story of the crossing of the Red Sea is read in some churches on the night before Easter. It reminds us of the possibility of crossing over from slavery to freedom, from death to life.

Fugitives and the sick

Cuthbert knew that all kinds of fugitives and runaways would come to Lindisfarne in the years after his death.[5] The monks gave them sanctuary for a while and negotiated with the authorities on their behalf. If you had been crossing the sands in those days, you would also have met people with disabilities and illnesses. Miracles were said to have taken place at Cuthbert's tomb. One day a cart crossed the island carrying a boy, strapped down, yelling and biting anyone who came near him. He was said to be 'possessed by an evil spirit'. In other words, the doctor had found no physical cause for his condition. The remedy probably owes more to faith and good nursing than to pharmacy, but it was based on the belief that the love of God can come to us through physical things. Near the monastery there was a patch of earth where the water had been thrown from the washing of Cuthbert's body. A few crumbs of this earth were dissolved in water and given to the boy to drink. He was better next morning.[6] It's important to note that neither the monks nor the patients relied on supernatural means alone. There were skilled physicians on the island and many people came to consult them as well as to pray for help. Not everyone asked for a physical cure. Clement, a visitor from the Netherlands, became seriously ill while staying at the abbey. His prayer was simply that God would either help him to get better or free him from his distress.[7] There's a note of desperation in this prayer, but there's also a kind of trust that, whatever happened, he would be all right.

Lindisfarne

After the dunes, the last half-mile into the village is through fertile-looking fields. There are still two families farming on the island but it isn't easy nowadays for local people to carry on their traditional occupations. In the 18th century, 24 households held land and grazing rights on Lindisfarne. The marram grass or 'bent' on the dunes was used as common grazing and they thatched their houses with it as well. There were two quarries and, by the 19th century, a lime kiln. Fishing was a major industry for a while. A visitor in 1859 saw 1400 barrels of herring down by the harbour, ready for export. While the men went out in the boats, the women worked at gutting and packing. All over town there were nets hanging out to dry and, at almost every door, heaps of floats and lines. There's little fishing today, but you can still see some of the boats down by the harbour, turned upside-down and converted into huts. Tourism is now the main source of work and native islanders face an uncertain future. In February 1998, there was only one child in the school and many of the houses have been sold at high prices or turned into holiday homes. Five new houses have been built recently for local families, but it's easy to see why they sometimes feel invaded by the outside world. Pilgrims are always welcome, but no one wants to be part of a living museum or holy theme park, so do try to be sensitive. In particular, please don't stare through people's windows, take intrusive photographs or trample on family graves in the churchyard.

Journey's end

Most pilgrimages have a focal point, but on Lindisfarne there's no one place which is obviously the 'end'. Sooner or later, all medieval pilgrims would have wanted to pray at the tomb of St Cuthbert. There they would lay down any burdens they had been carrying with them, ask for help, give thanks and pray for anyone who had asked for their prayers or whose welfare was dear to them. It was the custom to bring a gift as well. Normally this was a material gift, a votive offering of some kind, but then as now, there were probably some who offered the gift of themselves, nothing more or less. Cuthbert's tomb is long gone and there's no large basilica or cathedral, no one place which is supposedly holier than all the others. Perhaps this is a good thing. For most people it's enough just to soak up the atmosphere of the island.

Lindisfarne Priory.

Some say they feel a sense of 'presence' here. That may well be, but I can't help thinking that Cuthbert and Aidan would be disappointed if pilgrims came to the island looking for them or for some kind of mystical experience. Such experiences do happen, but straining after one is perhaps the surest way of losing touch with reality. There is a Taoist saying: 'Give up holiness, renounce sainthood and it will be a thousand times better for everyone.' A Christian equivalent might be 'Leave self behind', including that part of ourselves which craves extraordinary experiences. Like all true saints, Cuthbert and Aidan pointed beyond themselves, not seeking their own holiness, but opening themselves up to a greater reality.

Meeting up
If you want to mark the end of your pilgrimage in some way, it's as well to plan in advance. If you are travelling in a group you will need written permission to use any of the buildings on the island and/or the churchyard. (See 'Before You Set Out', p.25.) The Priory is a popular choice. It has lovely open views and is close to where St Cuthbert's tomb once was, but it has no roof so be prepared for all kinds of weather. There are also St Mary's parish church, the Roman Catholic church, the United Reformed church

and the village hall. The statue of St Aidan next to the Priory makes a good outdoor gathering place but, again, permission is needed as it is in the churchyard. This is mainly a matter of courtesy but it's also to avoid the awkwardness of several groups crowding into the same place at the same time, especially if islanders are also trying to use it, for a wedding, say, or a funeral. Visitors are welcome to join in with local prayers and church services. Morning and evening prayers are offered every day in St Mary's; there is morning prayer in the Catholic church most days; and an informal evening service in the United Reformed church on Saturday evenings. Check notice-boards for times and other events.

The Priory

The Priory church (open 10am–6pm or dusk, April to Oct; 10 am–4pm, Nov. to March) is thought to have been built on the site of the small seventh-century church which once housed St Cuthbert's tomb. This may have been at the east end of the church, where the chancel is now. The narrow passage between the chancel and the north transept may have been designed to let pilgrims visit the place where St Cuthbert's body had once rested, without walking through the choir area which was normally reserved for monks. The body had long since been removed to protect it from the Vikings. It was brought back to the island briefly between 1069 and 1070, this time to protect it from the Normans, but it was soon returned to Durham. The Priory was built later, in the 12th century.

The earliest pilgrims to Lindisfarne would have seen only a small church with a burial ground nearby, surrounded by the living quarters of the monks and various outbuildings. The monastery was no longer as basic as it had been in Aidan's day. The quality of the vestments found in Cuthbert's tomb shows that the monks could draw on considerable wealth for occasions like this, but the church buildings remained small. There were at least two, maybe more, on the island. One was destroyed by the Vikings in 793. Another was dismantled and taken to a safer site at Norham. This may have been an early church built by St Aidan, or the oak church built by his successor, Finán, 'after the Irish manner' with a thatch of reeds.[8] Later bishops dedicated it to St Peter and covered it with lead, to preserve it and make it more 'suitable' for an episcopal see. Cuthbert would have known this church and could probably have told us its original dedication. It seems to have become known as St Peter's only after the Synod of Whitby (p.46).

A church without a patron saint was like a family without a mother or a father, so it's hard to imagine Finán building his without dedicating it to some holy man or woman of the past. Perhaps he dedicated it to Aidan, but other monasteries founded from Iona (Durrow, Derry, Kells) looked to Columba as their patron saint, so that is another possibility. There's no proof either way. We may expect, however, that there would have been at least one dedication to Columba somewhere on the island and later records show that there was once a Columba's chapel and a Columba's street; and the farm north of the car park is called St Coombs, probably a derivative of Columba.[9]

St Mary's parish church

St Mary's, next to the Priory, may have been built on the site of an earlier church. The building you see today dates mainly from the 13th century but parts of it are certainly older. It is aligned with the Priory in a way which is typical of Anglo-Saxon monasteries, and some people think this was where Aidan's church once stood. There was a large stone cross outside St Mary's, at the east end. The socket is still there, between the church and the Priory steps. It's also known as the 'Petting Stone' and there's a tradition that any bride who can jump over it, helped by a fisherman on either side, is sure of a happy marriage.[10] Public worship goes on twice a day at St Mary's, year in year out. Visitors are welcome at all services and there's a pin-board where anyone can leave a request for prayer. St Mary's is not a 'museum of dead things' but it does have a small exhibition area, a good collection of leaflets and a facsimile of the Lindisfarne Gospels.

The Lindisfarne Gospels

This beautiful illuminated manuscript, one of the greatest treasures of 'dark age' Britain, is similar to the ninth-century Book of Kells, thought to have been created on Iona. The Lindisfarne Gospels were created here on the island around AD 700 'for God and for St Cuthbert'. The magnificent calligraphy was expertly done, in the Irish style, probably by Eadfrith, Bishop of Lindisfarne. In Ireland, the Book of Durrow was already in existence. Durrow was a Columban monastery and St Columba, sometimes known as 'Columba of the pens', had a reputation as a calligrapher himself, so it's possible that in Eadfrith we see the flowering of an art which had been brought to Lindisfarne from some other part of the Columban *familia* in the time of Aidan or soon afterwards. Some of the illustrations also show Mediterranean influence and the blue colour was made from lapis lazuli, from the foothills of the Himalayas. This was not a book for everyday use. It was probably brought out only on special occasions, but the stories and teachings which it enshrines were a daily source of inspiration to the people who lived and worked here.

St Cuthbert's Isle
The churchyard overlooks a tiny island where Cuthbert is said to have spent time alone in prayer, before withdrawing to the greater seclusion of Inner Farne (p.42). There is a cross on the island and the remains of a later medieval chapel. It's possible to walk across to them at low tide. This is one of the places where you may see eider ducks, known sometimes as 'Cuddy ducks' or 'St Cuthbert's chickens'. A leaflet about them in St Mary's church explains the association.[11] While they are nesting, eiders can appear to be very tame. One 12th-century account says that the Cuddy ducks of Lindisfarne used to nest in people's houses, on tables, under beds, even under the bedclothes. The presence of so many saints on the island was thought to have re-established a sort of harmony between them and human beings so that they were not afraid and would sometimes even allow people to touch them. Few of them nest on Lindisfarne today, but if you ever do happen on a sitting eider, please don't try to touch her. She may look calm and unruffled but what she's really doing is bravely protecting her eggs. Too much disturbance from human beings can drive her away.

There are more things to see and do on Lindisfarne than can easily be managed in one visit, especially if you want to keep the mood of pilgrimage. If you have time, the Museum (same opening hours as the Priory) is excellent and covers all aspects of island life. It houses a good collection of early carved stones, including one, from the late ninth century, with the sun and moon on either side of a cross on one side and a party of armed warriors on the other. The Castle (April to October only) was built in the 16th century to protect the coast and harbour from Scottish attack, but it was also a base for English raids into Scotland. Ten English warships and 2,200 soldiers landed here on their way to the 'rough wooing' (p.90) in the 1540s. The castle was restored by Sir Edwin Lutyens in 1903 and is worth a visit. It is now owned by the National Trust. The interiors have a fairy-tale quality about them and you can look out of the little windows onto the North Sea, as from the cabins of a ship. There is also a small garden nearby by Gertrude Jekyll.

If the heritage industry gets too much, the north side of the island is the place to make for. Between Emanuel Head and Snipe Point there are some quiet beaches and the walk through the dunes is pleasant. Look out for wild orchids in the grass between May and August. Holy Island is part of the Lindisfarne National Nature Reserve and you can expect to see a wide range of birds, particularly in winter and during the spring and autumn migrations. These include large numbers of ducks and waders, whooper swans, and a small rare population of pale-bellied brent geese from Spitzbergen which winter in Denmark but come to Holy Island when it gets too cold over there.

Staying over and getting back
Remember to check the tide-table again for your return journey and plan it as carefully as your journey out. There are various places to stay on the island but they can all get extremely busy, so don't expect to be able find accommodation at short notice. No camping is allowed. If you don't want to walk back, the community minibus (p.25) may take you, especially if you arrange it in advance.

⊕ *Parking can be difficult in the village, even with an orange badge. If possible, come at a quiet time. For the last few years, summer visitors have been asked to park in the field on the left at the entrance to the village. Orange-badge holders may use the coach park which is a little nearer the centre, next to the Lindisfarne Hotel. From there it is about 350 yds to the Priory, museum and St Mary's church. There are accessible toilets in the car park but they are kept locked so you will need to bring your own Radar key (p.23). There is another accessible toilet in St Cuthbert's Church Centre. Surface in the car park is hard-packed gravel; tarmac from there to the museum, Priory and St Mary's church. There is a dropping-off point about 20 yds from the Priory/museum ticket office, for cars only. The Priory is about 100 yds beyond the ticket office and St Mary's church about 50 yds beyond that. You do not need a ticket for St Mary's and can see the Priory well from the churchyard.*

● *Priory: 4–10 steps down into the nave. Ten more into cloister. Ramps available but 'this may change'. Gradient – path to the Priory is level; ground level once inside. Surface – grass, uneven. Viewpoints clear. No passing places. No seats.*

● *Museum: level entry, no steps. Seats – about 4–5 upright chairs without arms.*

● *St Mary's church: if you are not visiting the Priory or the museum, you can use a different entrance with a nearer dropping-off point. Continue south from Fiddlers Green, look for the side gate into churchyard. Ramp. Gate and path are narrow. Hard surface. No passing places. Distance from gate to church – about 70 yds. Gradient – level. Five steps down into church. Seats – pews.*

● *St Cuthbert's Isle: best unobstructed view is from turning place above Jenny Bell's Well. Access to island difficult. Not recommended.*

● *Castle: access is difficult. Not recommended.*

Notes

1   Presumably across the sands at the mouth of the Tweed.

2   P. Hume Brown, *Early Travellers in Scotland*, Edinburgh, 1973, 24–9.

3   Exodus 14.

4   Exodus 1,5.

5   Bede, *Life*, 37

6   op.cit.41; Anon., 15.

7   Anon., 16. Bede, *Life*, 44.

8   Bede, *EH*, 3.25.

9   Deirdre O'Sullivan, 'The Plan of the Early Christian Monastery on Lindisfarne', *CCC*, 140–1.

10 Frank Graham, *Holy Island*, 25.

11 'St Cuthbert's Ducks: the Eider Duck of the Farnes', Marygate House, 1981.

Going on a Pilgrimage

The pilgrim instinct

Pilgrimage is one of the most ancient and widespread of all religious activities. There are pilgrimages to Jerusalem and Rome, Mecca and Varanasi, to mountains in Japan and the Andes, to rocks in the Australian desert and rivers in Africa. Pilgrimages are older than Christianity, older than Judaism, but they were adopted by both. Mount Zion seems to have been a holy mountain long before the Hebrews arrived there, but it was to become the site of their holiest place, the temple in Jerusalem, which they visited three times a year for the great pilgrim festivals of Passover, Pentecost and Tabernacles. We still have some of their pilgrim songs:

> *How lovely is your dwelling place, O Lord of hosts!*
> *I pine, I faint with longing for the courts*
> *of the Lord's temple...* [1]

It's likely that Mary and Joseph heard songs like these when they travelled up to Jerusalem, with their neighbours and their young son, for the feast of the Passover. When he grew up, Jesus made the same journey with his disciples.[2] Later, Jerusalem became a place of pilgrimage for Christians and Moslems as well. It was one of the oldest and most popular destinations for Christian pilgrimages, but it was a long way from northern Europe and, in the course of the Middle Ages, other centres were established closer to people's homes. In some of these, Christian shrines were built on or near the sites of pre-Christian ones. People continued to visit them as holy places, but with a different understanding of what they were doing.

The practice of pilgrimage was rejected at the Reformation but it survived in some places and also in the image of the spiritual journey. Psalms like the one above were given a 'spiritual' interpretation and new songs were written on the pilgrimage theme:

> *Whither, children, are you going,*
> *going each with staff in hand?*
> *We are going on a journey, going to a better land.*[3]

I remember singing this in Sunday School, all dressed up to greet the new minister, girls in best frocks, boys in white shirts and ties, some of them in kilts. We were learning that the whole of life was a pilgrimage and that our final destination was with God in heaven. We had little idea of what that journey might mean, but we felt brave and intrepid. We got the same feeling from that other famous hymn, 'To be a Pilgrim' by John Bunyan, in which we promised not to be daunted by 'hobgoblins' or 'foul fiends'. Being a pilgrim seemed like a lot of fun. It had a feel-good factor.

We were not the first people to notice this, of course. Some of the pilgrims in Chaucer's *Canterbury Tales* are clearly in holiday mood as they set out, with the first breath of spring, to combine pleasure with a more serious purpose. Not everyone is comfortable with this combination, but there's nothing po-faced about the old pilgrim songs: 'Come into his presence with singing...' says the Psalmist, 'enter his gates with thanksgiving and his courts with praise'.[4] Light-hearted or serious, pilgrimage has long been regarded as a powerful exercise for body and soul, capable of leading people into situations which they might avoid or miss in everyday life. These situations can be refreshing or challenging but the challenge, the difficulty of pilgrimage, is a traditional part of it. At times, it has even been thought of as a kind of martyrdom.

Into the unknown

Cuthbert would have grown up with this idea of pilgrimage. He would have known that some people make pilgrimages to specific places, but his Irish training would have familiarised him with open-ended pilgrimages as well. St Columba had left Ireland 'to be a pilgrim for Christ', choosing what the Irish called 'white martyrdom' or martyrdom without blood. Earlier generations of Christians had died for their beliefs at the hands of the Roman imperial authorities. Columba laid down his life in a different way, by leaving behind much that was comfortable and familiar in the north of Ireland and setting off in his middle years for Scottish Dál Riada, in Argyll, and the boundaries of Pictland. He may have had some idea of what to expect there, but it was still a journey of faith and he probably did not know exactly where he would end up. It's possible that Aidan and Boisil saw their missions to Lindisfarne and Melrose in a similar light. There were some who took greater risks still, and set off on pilgrimages with no fixed destination. At the end of the ninth century, three Irish men were washed up on the shores of Cornwall, having set off in a boat without oars 'because they wanted for the love of God to be abroad, they did not care where'.[5]

Other pilgrimages of faith

Abraham has sometimes been seen as the first pilgrim in this sense. In the book of Genesis, he and Sarah, his wife, leave their country and their own people and set out in trust for a land which they believe God will show them.[6] Abraham later became an important role-model for the first Christians. Sometimes they had to leave home because of persecution, but more often it was an inner pilgrimage which they faced. The comfortable homeland of their old beliefs and attitudes no longer corresponded with their experience and they found themselves breaking new ground, travelling into new spiritual territory.[7] To St Paul, Abraham was the great example of faith in the Hebrew Bible; but the greatest influence on his life was someone of his own time and culture, Jesus of Nazareth, who had left his workshop and the synagogue of his youth to become a wandering rabbi with 'nowhere to lay his head'. His pilgrimage was not, ultimately, the holy city but the 'kingdom of God'. This can be understood in an otherworldly way to mean heaven/the hereafter, but it seems from the Gospels that when Jesus spoke about 'the kingdom of God' he meant something which was already happening here and now. God's way for the world was a present reality to him, now as well as in the future. He wanted people to know about it. Indeed, he went about proclaiming it and being a living example of it, inviting others to do the same. Not everyone was meant to respond by giving up everything and leaving home. Jesus does not tell Martha to sell the house where she made him welcome, and when the man known as Legion wants to follow him, he tells him to go home to his friends instead.[8] However, pilgrimages with no fixed destination can be seen as responses to this passionate invitation of Jesus, to follow him in living God's way.

Pilgrimages to holy places
Alongside these open-ended pilgrimages was the ancient custom of visiting holy places. These were also pilgrimages of faith, involving a much less radical renunciation than the other kind, but they could be demanding none the less. It was common for people to make a will before setting off. Travelling was much more dangerous in those days and not everyone expected to return. They would also put their affairs in order and make peace with anyone they had fallen out with. By the end of the fourth century, if not earlier, British Christians were visiting holy places in the Mediterranean world.[9] Pilgrimages to the Holy Land had been made before, but they became more popular all round when the Empress Helena visited in AD 326 and 'discovered' the 'true cross'; and when her son, the Emperor Constantine, built the Church of the Holy Sepulchre on the site soon afterwards. Accounts of St Jerome's experiences in Antioch, Syria, Egypt and Bethlehem had a similar effect and soon guides, hostels and a whole pilgrimage industry were getting under way. Arculf, a Gallic bishop who had made the pilgrimage, visited Iona in the early 680s. Adomnán the abbot, was clearly fascinated and quickly put Arculf's descriptions into a book, *De Locis Sanctis/On the Holy Places*. When he visited Northumbria, just before Cuthbert's death, he brought a copy with him and presented it to the king.[10]

The pilgrimage to Rome centred mainly around the tombs of

St Peter and St Paul, believed to have been martyred there, along with large numbers of other Christians whose tombs could also be visited. Several of Cuthbert's contemporaries made the journey. These included Benedict and Ceolfrid, Abbots of Wearmouth and Jarrow, Wilfrid, who was a lay person on his first visit, and several Anglo-Saxon kings. Cadwalla, king of the West Saxons, went there to be baptised and died soon afterwards. Bede saw this as a good thing. To die in a holy place was considered a great blessing and many people believed that it would be helpful, at the end of time, to be found in company with a saint. Some deliberately went on pilgrimage towards the end of their lives, looking for exactly such a 'place of resurrection'. Bede also says that in England, in the aftermath of the Synod of Whitby (p.37) all kinds of people vied with one another to make the pilgrimage to Rome: 'both noble and simple, layfolk and clergy, men and women alike'.[11]

Gradually, however, Christian shrines became more established locally. There had always been holy places in Britain and Ireland, some of them pre-Christian in origin, but now they became associated with Christian saints. From the fifth century, possibly earlier, there was a pilgrimage to the tomb of St Alban, a third-century Briton executed in the Roman city of Verulamium, north of London. St Germanus, visiting from the Continent in 429, paid his respects there, taking away earth from the tomb and leaving the relics of other martyrs as a gift. By Bede's day, there was a beautiful church at St Alban's 'where sick folk are healed and frequent miracles take place'.[12] In Ireland, by the end of the seventh century, 'numberless people' were apparently flocking to the tomb of St Brigit in Kildare – 'some for the abundant feasting, others for the healing of their afflictions, others to watch the pageant of the crowds, others with great gifts and offerings'.[13] The pilgrimage to Cuthbert's tomb on Lindisfarne was getting under way at the same time, part of a wave of new pilgrimages to the tombs of Anglo-Saxon saints including Oswald (p.141), Etheldreda (p.119) and Chad.[14]

Healing

Many people went to Lindisfarne in search of healing (p.150). This was a common reason for pilgrimages everywhere. It was linked with a cult of relics which can seem strange, even gruesome, to us today, but it was part of an integrated world-view in which it was believed that holiness, the presence of God, can somehow permeate the physical world and be available to people there. The bodies of saints, especially martyrs, were believed to retain something of this vital presence, even after death, and to be sources of healing and protection.

Cuthbert was not a martyr in the original sense, but he came to be seen as one. The Anonymous Life calls him 'martyr' and also 'confessor', that is, someone who witnesses to the faith publicly, at great cost to him or herself.[15] These titles were probably given to him because of the circumstances of his death and also because, from an early age, he was believed to have surrendered his life completely in other ways. People hoped that by praying at his tomb they might be affected by his holiness. They also asked Cuthbert to pray for them, something which not all Christians recognise as legitimate today.

In medieval times, it was almost impossible for ordinary people, let alone the sick and the marginalised, to approach directly the powerful men (and it was mostly men) who shaped and governed their lives. They had to find a sponsor or patron to do it for them. How much more so, they reasoned, when approaching God, the 'King of kings'. There is enormous reverence in this approach, and it was often in a spirit of reverence and humility that people made it. However, there was also a sense that God was 'no for the likes o' us'. The normal liturgy of the church was in Latin; the high altar was often hidden behind a screen, and was in a part of the church reserved for the clergy, monks or nuns. Few people went regularly to communion. The reliquaries of saints, on the other hand, could be seen and even touched, and pilgrims could offer their own prayers beside them. This is very different from the prayer taught by Jesus in the Gospels where he calls God, 'Abba/father' and teaches people to approach 'him' not like a human ruler (king, queen, prime minister, president) but like the kind of parent everyone would like to have: welcoming, wise, generous and forgiving.[16] In the Catholic and Orthodox churches, however, many people still ask the saints to pray for them, not as an alternative to God, but in the same way as they would ask a friend or a religious community.

Reconciliation

Pilgrimage was sometimes prescribed like a medicine to people whose lives had gone seriously wrong in other ways. Fugitives from justice began arriving at Cuthbert's tomb almost at once (p.150). We are not told that they had been sent by anyone in particular. Possibly, to begin with, they were simply claiming the right of sanctuary. Later, people who claimed this right in Durham Cathedral were allowed to stay for 37 days while their case was decided. They were given a black garment to wear with a yellow St Cuthbert's cross on the shoulder. If they were found guilty, they might be sent on a penitential pilgrimage to a particular shrine, or into exile, which, as we have seen, could also be a form of pilgrimage. They were then given 'the cloak of St Cuthbert' and a white wooden cross to carry. This marked them out as criminals, but it also gave them a measure of protection as no one was supposed to harm them while they were doing penance.[17]

One early example of a penitential pilgrimage is found in Adomnán's *Life of Saint Columba*. A young man, Librán, turns up on Iona, dressed as a monk. Columba finds him sitting in the guest house on his own and asks him about himself. Librán tells him that he comes from Connacht in the West of Ireland, and has 'made the effort of the long journey in order to wipe out his sins on a pilgrimage'. He eventually confesses that he has killed a man, been bailed out by a relative, promised to work for him for the rest of his life, then run off to Iona. Columba prescribes seven years in the penitential colony on Tiree, and helps with his rehabilitation afterwards.[18]

There are other early examples from the Irish tradition, but penitential pilgrimage to specific places did not really take off on the continent till the ninth century.[19] When it did, it was initially only a penance for serious crimes like murdering one's father or a close relative. Stealing from churches and offences against priests, monks and nuns fell into the same category. No one was above the law in this respect. In the 11th and 12th centuries, dukes, kings, emperors, archbishops, all were sent on penitential pilgrimages for various reasons. By the 13th century, pilgrimage was being prescribed for less serious crimes. The Inquisition sometimes sent people on pilgrimages for their unorthodox views. Local rulers were asked to help in ensuring that such penances were carried out, and in some places, in the Netherlands for example, the civil authorities themselves started sentencing people to pilgrimages, for crimes ranging from murder to fraud, idleness and breach of the peace. Most pilgrimages, however, were prescribed by the Church, following confession, as part of the sacrament of Penance or Reconciliation as it is now called. They were seen as a way of tackling, while here on earth, some of the suffering which was believed to await people in purgatory as a result of their sins. This gave rise to all kinds of fears and abuses as we shall see but, at their best, penitential pilgrimages were intended to provide a way for people to be reconciled, in this life, with God, with themselves and with the rest of society.

Devotional pilgrimages

People have probably always had mixed motives for going on pilgrimages. We have already seen how the crowds at St Brigit's in Kildare included some who came mainly for the food and the festive atmosphere. Medieval pilgrimage could be 'a custom, a habit, an escape and an entertainment' but it could also be 'an act of profound faith'.[21] Appearances can be deceptive. Even the most frivolous-looking pilgrim might be carrying their faith about them secretly, like a love-letter, or be giddy with the simple joy of being alive. It was not uncommon to go on pilgrimage after a brush with death. Aeneus Sylvius (p.147) was one of these, though he was not exactly happy trudging through East Lothian in midwinter, in his bare feet. It would be interesting to know more about the ordinary reasons for pilgrimages, but the vast majority of pilgrims left no record of their thoughts or feelings and might not have cared to share them with strangers in any case. Those who were writing at the time tell us mainly about pilgrims whose motives were officially recorded or could be guessed at (criminals, people with disabilities) so it's difficult to get a clear idea of what was going on in the hearts and minds of ordinary pilgrims. If there are people today who go to Lindisfarne or Iona, Lourdes or Galilee out of genuine devotion, it seems reasonable to assume that there were similar people in medieval times.

Pilgrimage and community

Going on a pilgrimage often has the effect of bringing people together. The demands of the journey and the sense of common purpose can help to foster a deep sense of community among pilgrims. This can be used in positive and negative ways. Pilgrimage still sometimes creates solidarity among a particular group to the exclusion of others. St Paul had a vision of unity beyond distinctions of race, class and gender[22] but it's all too easy for pilgrimages to become a rallying point for division. There is, for example, a very emotive Serbian pilgrimage to Kosovo, and in England pilgrimages to St Cuthbert's tomb were once deployed to boost the morale of soldiers bound for the Border wars.

In 934, during the struggle for control of Northumbria, Athelstan, king of Wessex and York, made a pilgrimage to St Cuthbert's tomb at Chester-le-Street. He was on his way north with an invading army. He claimed sovereignty over the 'men of Alba' and was about to enforce it by laying waste to the east coast as far north as Dunnottar.[23] Ten years later, his brother Edmund made the same pilgrimage for similar reasons. The 17th-century historian Robert Hegg says that Edmund was making use of his soldiers' belief that St Cuthbert was 'a tutelary Deitie against the Scotts'. Confident in his protection, 'they were much encouraged, to the grave disadvantage of their enemies'.[24] There is probably an element of exaggeration here. The soldiers would never have called Cuthbert a 'tutelary Deitie' (guardian god) but they would have believed or wanted to believe in the saint's protection and it's very likely that Edmund made use of this.

Scottish kings laid claim to Cuthbert too. After all, he had lived and worked in the Borders which was disputed territory in Edmund's day.[25] When the foundation stone of Durham Cathedral was laid in 1093, the Scottish king, Malcolm III (St Margaret's husband) was there to see it. His three sons, Edgar, Alexander I and David I, all supported the building works and made pilgrimages to St Cuthbert's tomb there.[26] It was this same David who invited the Cistercians to Melrose, with all its Cuthbert associations.

David's visit to Durham provides another example of a restricted community. At some stage, a tradition had grown up that Cuthbert did not like or associate with women. This was quite untrue. The Lives show him in the company of women and men, but by the 12th century his pilgrimage had become a men-only affair and women were not allowed anywhere near the feretory or shrine area where his body was kept. A serving woman in David's retinue is said to have disguised herself as a man and been struck down as she crossed into the forbidden area.[27] There are other stories of the same kind, and visitors to the cathedral can still see the line at the back of the church which women were not allowed to cross. Nowadays, of course, they may even see women at the altar.

When the Crusades came to be seen as another kind of pilgrimage (p.57) they too created an in-group and an out-group. Knights, adventurers and penitents bonded together to save their souls and recapture Jerusalem from the Moslems. In 1095, Pope Urban offered a plenary indulgence to crusaders, that is, a certificate promising total exemption from the pains of purgatory. Many saw this as an attractive offer. It carried the possibility of winning lands and booty in this life as well as heaven in the life to come. This kind of 'holy war' was seen as quite acceptable, even glorious, at the time, though it shames us now.

In 1997, a pilgrimage took place which tried to overcome some of the divisions of the past. The occasion was the 1400th anniversary of the death of St Columba, and of the arrival in Canterbury of St Augustine, the Roman missionary. Pilgrims set off from Rome and travelled, by way of Canterbury, to Iona, taking in various other Celtic foundations on the way, including Lindisfarne and Melrose. Pilgrims also arrived from Donegal, and Mary Robinson, President of the Irish Republic, spoke in Iona Abbey about the need for reconciliation, especially in Northern Ireland. All kinds of divided communities came together here, mainly under religious labels (for example, Presbyterian, Roman Catholic, Anglican, Episcopalian) but involving people from different countries, regions and cultures as well. For a few days, they lived what Victor and Edith Turner have called an 'alternative idealised community' – not without problems or friction, but community none the less, and one which aimed to be inclusive.

Reasons to stay at home

It is said that an Irish teacher called Dairchellach was once thinking of going on a pilgrimage. He went to see his soul-friend, Samthann, who usually helped him with such decisions. 'Don't do it,' she's said to have replied. Did she see before her a capable person trying to avoid his responsibilities? Or a restless person looking for a change of scene? Her answer provides the only clue: 'God is near to all who seek him,' she said.[28] Perhaps it was years since Dairchellach had felt the presence of God; perhaps news of the great holy places where Jesus and his disciples had actually walked made him feel contemptuous of local sanctuaries. We can only guess, but what Samthann seems to be saying to him is this: 'God is with you here and now, in your own culture, in your own everyday life. You don't have to go looking for him in distant times and places or in sacred sites. Settle down.' Over the centuries there have been many who would have agreed with her. Pilgrimages have been described variously as unnecessary, escapist, even as a kind of unholy scam. At times, all these things have undoubtedly been true.

Like any human enterprise, pilgrimage can go wrong as well as right. It had always had its critics, but by the late Middle Ages educated opinion was turning against it, not just in the universities but among literate townspeople as well.[29] A trade in bogus relics meant that many shrines contained objects which were literally beyond belief: pieces of the burning bush, milk of the Virgin Mary, the duplicated body parts of saints. Kings and churchmen amassed huge collections. By 1520, Martin Luther's protector, Frederick of Saxony, had over 19,000 pieces. Relics were sometimes stolen by one abbey from another. This is probably how the bones of the Venerable Bede came to be in Durham.[30] Faith can go to work on all kinds of things, but as the dishonesty of the relic-traders came to light, so scepticism grew.

Another abuse concerned penitential pilgrimages. From the 11th century, but commonly during the 14th and 15th, these could be done vicariously, even posthumously. In other words, it was no longer necessary to do your penance yourself. To begin with, vicarious pilgrimages were mainly undertaken by friends and relatives, but gradually a class of professional pilgrims grew up to service the needs of those who were too busy, too lazy or simply dead. It was similar with pilgrimages of healing. At the end of the 14th century, a professional pilgrim known as *le pélerin du roi* was constantly on the road in France and over the border to Compostela in Spain, praying for the recovery of the French king, Charles VI, who was suffering from a mental illness.[31] There's something touching about the selflessness of those who went on vicarious pilgrimages for family and friends, but people were beginning to ask questions. Did pilgrimages really do what they were claimed to do? Did they work? Of course, the guardians of churches and businesspeople along the route had a vested interest in the matter. Pilgrims needed to be fed and housed but they were, on the whole, profitable. Their gifts brought beauty and prestige to the shrines they visited.

The great Christian humanist Erasmus (c.1469–1536) reminded people that it was more important to imitate Christ and his saints than to go dashing about on pilgrimages. A brilliant satirist, he made fun of the idea that heaven could be bought through offerings and indulgences, but he still believed in the friendship and protection of the saints. 'A saint will take care of you if you imitate him,' he wrote. For Erasmus, pilgrimages could still be worthwhile if they were done in the right spirit, for the love of God and with a genuine desire to live a better life.[32] Even as he wrote, however, others were taking a harder line.

Objections of the Reformers

'The true Christian pilgrimage is not to Rome or Compostela, but to the prophets, the Psalms, and the Gospels.'[33] Martin Luther (1483–1546) had lost all faith in pilgrimages and this is the kind of pronouncement you might have heard over the dinner table in the Luther household in the early days of the Reformation. Since the invention of the printing press, the Bible had become more widely available than ever before and had appeared in translation for the first time in centuries. Scholars like Luther had become aware of how much the Church had changed since New Testament times. Change can, of course, be a part of normal, healthy development, a way of meeting and adapting to new situations, but Luther saw nothing but decline and corruption in the medieval Church.

Pilgrimages were not the main focus of his attack. It was much more radical than that. But, in returning to the scriptures, he undermined many of the traditional reasons for pilgrimage and called a halt to it over large areas of northern Europe.

He did not do this single-handedly of course. Reformers like Ulrich Zwingli, John Calvin and John Knox and Radicals like the Anabaptists took a similar view. There are important differences between these various groups but they shared a common desire to be more like the early Christians, more rooted in scripture and more directly in touch with God. Saints came to be seen as unnecessary, obstructive rather than helpful. Some were allowed to remain as role models, but not as heavenly patrons. The main focus was to be on God and the life and work of Jesus.

This alone would have weakened the medieval feeling for pilgrimage, but there was more to come. Everyone, Protestants and Catholics alike, believed that something had gone wrong with the world since God created it. Its goodness had been spoiled, and it was generally agreed that human beings had contributed to this. The argument was over what, if anything, could be done about it. Both sides agreed that humans needed to acknowledge their mistakes. Under the old system, this was followed by absolution and then penance which could involve a lot of hardship and effort. Luther argued that this last stage was unnecessary. People still had to confess their sins but then God would forgive them fully and freely. Penance was done away with, as was the doctrine of purgatory.

The relief which followed was based, paradoxically, on a more pessimistic view of human nature. Human efforts towards goodness were not just unnecessary in the Reformers' view, they were hopelessly misguided. Men and women, they argued, are quite incapable of contributing to their own salvation. The life, death and resurrection of Jesus put things right once and for all, making all kinds of religious activities ('works') redundant, including pilgrimages.

Close-down and survival

There were those who regretted their demise, but many people experienced the Reformation as hugely liberating: no more fear of purgatory, no more lifetime of anxious effort. Other worries crept

in after a while, but as far as pilgrimage was concerned it had lost
its theological basis and no one came forward with a new one. The
abbeys, many of which had been pilgrimage-centres, were closed
down (monasticism being seen as a 'work' too) and in Protestant
countries pilgrimage came quickly to an end.

The Catholic Church did not stand still through all of this.
Change was under way there too. The Council of Trent (1545–63)
rejected most of the Reformers' criticisms, but it provided a solid
basis for renewal and for tackling abuses within the Church. The
Council did not accept that people are incapable of goodness. They
were not expected to succeed fully without God's help, but they
were expected to cooperate in the process by receiving the sacraments, giving alms, fasting and doing good works as before. This
meant, of course, that pilgrimage still had a place. So it survived
and continues in an unbroken tradition in many parts of Europe
and the Third World. The ordinary Sunday liturgy is still seen as the
normal way to God (and of course it is much more accessible now)
but pilgrimage remains as an optional extra. There are still people
who go on harsh penitential pilgrimages of their own free will. The
pilgrimage to Station Island on Lough Derg in Donegal, is a good
example. But, even then, there are often other reasons: prayers for
a particular person or situation or simple devotion.

Revival

Pilgrimage went underground in Scotland, England and Wales, but
it was impossible to eradicate and survived as a metaphor for the
Christian life in the minds of people like John Bunyan and Sir
Walter Raleigh:

> *Bring me my scallop-shell of quiet,*
> *My staff of faith to walk upon,*
> *My scrip of joy, immortal diet,*
> *My bottle of salvation,*
> *My gown of glory, hope's true gage,*
> *And thus I'll take my pilgrimage...*

Like Bunyan, Raleigh was thinking about a spiritual journey, the
journey of the soul. He wrote this poem at a time when he was in
prison, on trial for his life.[34] Pilgrimages as physical journeys

would be back, however. At the end of the 18th century and the beginning of the 19th, the Romantic movement helped to create a new wave of interest in the medieval world, and William Wordsworth and Sir Walter Scott were among those who found inspiration in ruined abbeys like Tintern and Melrose. It was in this climate that the Oxford Movement began within Anglicanism and later the Church Service Society in the Church of Scotland. When, in 1931, a new Anglican chapel was built at Walsingham, the medieval pilgrimage there was revived. Thousands of Anglicans and Catholics now make the journey every year. By the 1950s, the Iona Community was providing for visitors a regular – and demanding – pilgrimage around Iona, led by staff from the abbey and involving symbolic actions and prayers at certain points. Some people are still uneasy about pilgrimage on theological grounds but there are signs that new understandings of pilgrimage are now being explored within the Protestant tradition. One example of this trend is the recently published anthology of new and traditional writings about pilgrimage, *Sacred Places, Pilgrim Paths* by Martin Robinson, director of mission and theology for the Bible Society.

Spiritual tourism?

Some pilgrimage centres like Compostela and Iona, Lindisfarne and Glastonbury now attract visitors from all religious backgrounds and none. St Cuthbert's Way is in a similar category, having been set up originally as a walking holiday rather than a traditional pilgrimage. Occasionally, we hear this dismissed as 'spiritual tourism' and certainly there are similarities between tourism and pilgrimage. Of course, some people are happy to describe themselves as spiritual tourists. They honestly admit that they do not feel at home in any one spiritual tradition and are simply looking around. This can become a kind of pilgrimage in itself. Unless they declare themselves, the difference between 'real' pilgrims and others is invisible to the naked eye. There's a wonderful example of this in the Hebrew Bible, where Eli, priest of Shiloh, sees a woman acting strangely in the temple and takes her to be a drunk. There is a pilgrim festival going on outside and he assumes that she is a 'spiritual tourist', someone who is not taking the occasion seriously. He could not be more wrong. This is

Hannah, mother of Samuel, praying desperately for a child. Eli soon realises his mistake and has the grace to admit it.[35]

The criticism is nothing new, however. 'If you go to the Holy Places out of curiosity,' said one 12th-century writer, 'the only benefit you will get is to have seen some pretty countryside.'[36] Pretty countryside is almost certainly being underestimated here. If God waits for us anywhere, is it only in the 'holy' place at the end of the road? But the concern is understandable: we might well be missing out on something important if our journey becomes simply one sight-seeing experience after another. Perhaps we need to recover something of the original meaning of holidays as 'holy days' – not fun in a strait-jacket, but special times of celebration. Holidays take us away, temporarily, from our normal everyday concerns; they make it possible for us to act differently, recover lost parts of ourselves, try out new experiences, get things back into perspective, go home renewed and refreshed. The theory with pilgrimages is that they go a step further, being consciously open to deeper levels of renewal and re-creation.[37] Perhaps, to adopt a famous advertising slogan, pilgrimages refresh the parts which ordinary holidays can't reach.

The inner journey
'Perhaps the interior way is the one that counts in the end. No journey can be more dark and difficult, unexpected and hazardous than that.'[38] This is the comment of a late 20th-century pilgrim, not a practising church-goer, but an observer whose personal quest is inseparable from her observations. Jennifer Lash was recovering from cancer when she made her pilgrimage through France to Compostela in Spain. She went, she says, in response to 'a hidden current (which) seeks, stirs, hides and yearns' within everyone.[39] Parts of the journey she loved, others she found painful and difficult: not least when her own hesitations met the confident assertions of others.

All new situations can be journeys of self-discovery, and pilgrimages can be so in a particularly powerful way. They present difficulties (physical discomfort, getting lost, disagreements) and delights (moments of unexpected joy, friendships, hidden strengths) and can cause people to shift their ground inwardly as well as on the physical path. It's easy to get the impression, from some kinds of popular spirituality, that self-knowledge is an end in itself. Most traditional religions take a different view. Even in Hinduism and Buddhism where nothing is more sacred than the Self, capital S, this is not to be confused with the individual personality.[40] In Christianity, too, it is important to know yourself: 'Learn to understand yourselves and take pity on yourselves!' writes St Teresa of Avila.[41] But that is only the beginning of the Christian life. The perfection of it, the most enduring part according to St Paul, is love. Knowledge, for all its value and effectiveness, is not even in second place.[42]

It is unlikely that Cuthbert could have spent years in prayer and solitude, living in community and dealing closely with people in distress without getting to know himself quite well, especially his own strengths and weaknesses. We may assume that self-knowledge was part of his experience, but it was only ever a means to an end. To love God and our neighbour (the two greatest commandments, in Mark's Gospel) we are told to go a step further. Jesus puts it very dramatically: 'If anyone wants to be a follower of mine, let him deny himself and take up his cross and follow me, for whoever wishes to save his life will lose it... '[43] This sounds extremely demanding, and it has taken some people well beyond what they would ever have expected of themselves. Not that self-denial is the same for everyone, of course. A timid person might be called upon to deny him- or herself in a different way from someone who enjoys power and status. But in traditional Christian theology God gives people the ability to change and the promise that it is all worthwhile: 'whoever loses his life for my sake will find it'. Perhaps pilgrimage can be a way of opening ourselves to that transformation: through self-knowledge to self-abandonment, to real life.

Your pilgrimage

So there it is. Pilgrimage through the ages. Some of the destinations have changed, as have some of the reasons for it. Perhaps your pilgrimage is a holiday, first and foremost. Perhaps your main interest is in history or in people and the countryside. You may be on pilgrimage for one of the traditional reasons with something particular on your mind, or simply for the love of God; a regular church-goer or one of the many people who believe in something but cannot define it or bring themselves to go to church; perhaps you are an atheist or a neo-pagan or a Buddhist, Jew, Sikh, Hindu or Moslem, exploring St Cuthbert's Way from a non-Christian perspective. Maybe you do not really know why you are on pilgrimage and are waiting to find out.

Notes

1 Psalm 84.1

2 Luke 2.41–43. Mk.10.32; 11.11; Mtt.21.; Lk.19. 28–48; Jn.12.12–15.

3 *Redemption Songs*, no. 681, author not found.

4 Psalm 100.

5 *The Anglo-Saxon Chronicle*, ed. Michael Swanton, London, 1996, 82. The voyage of Cormac, described in Adomnán's *Life of St Columba* is not described as a pilgrimage but as a search for 'a place of retreat on the ocean'. None the less, it has some of the same outward characteristics. See Adomnán's *Life of St Columba*, ed. Richard Sharpe, 2.42 and p.343, note 327.

6 Genesis, 12.1–6.

7 Romans 4; Galatians, 3–4.

8 Lk.10.38–42; Mk.5.19.

9 Pelagius, for example, travelled to Rome in the 380s and then on to Jerusalem by way of North Africa.

10 Adomnán, *Life of St Columba*, 2.46.

11 Bede, *EH* 4.18; 3.25; 5.7. Also several bishops or future bishops, e.g. Mellitus, Bede *EH* 2.4, and Oftfor 4.23.

12 Bede, *EH* I.7; Life of St Germanus of Auxerre.

13 Cogitosus, *Life of Saint Brigit*, §32, ed. S. Connolly and J.-M. Picard, *Journal of the Royal Society of Antiquaries of Ireland* 117, 1987.

14 Bede, EH 3..9–13; 4.19; 4.4.

15 Anon. *Life* XVI, including chapter heading.

16 Mtt.7.9–10. Parallels in Luke, Mark, John, James and 1 John. Also Lk.15.11–24.

17 *Sanctuarium Dunelmense*, Surtees Society V., ed. J. Raine, quoted by Hall in *EMP*, 99. Also C.J. Stranks, *This Sumptuous Church*, 33–4.

18 *Life of Saint Columba*, II.39.

19 Sigal, *Les Marcheurs de Dieu*, 16–18. Other early examples include the penance of Macuil Moccugreccae, *St Patrick: his writings and Muirchú's Life*, ed. A.B.E. Hood, London, 1978, 93–94, §23, and the penance for a woman murderer in Adomnán's Law. *Cáin Adamnáin, an Old-Irish treatise on the Law of Adamnán*, ed. Meyer, *Anecdota Oxoniensia*, Oxford, 1905, §45.

20 Sigal, *Marcheurs*, 20–3.

21 D.J. Hall, *English Medieval Pilgrimage*, London, 1966, 1.

22 Galatians 3.26–28.

23 Lynch, *Scotland*, 45.

24 *Legend of St Cuthbert*. Hegge, 1663, quoted in Hall, *English Medieval Pilgrimage*, 88.

25 The south-eastern boundary of Scotland reached something like its modern position, following the battle of Carham around 1018.

26 C. J. Stranks, *This Sumptuous Church: the Story of Durham Cathedral*, revised ed., London, 1993, 6. Peter Yeoman, *Pilgrimage in Medieval Scotland*, Edinburgh, 1999, 112.

27 Yeoman, ibid.

28 *Life of St Samthann of Clonbroney*, ed. Charles Plummer, *Vitae Sanctorium Hiberniae* II, 260, xxiv; Peter O'Dwyer, 'Celtic Monks and the Culdee Reform' in James P. Mackey, *An Introduction to Celtic Christianity*, Edinburgh, 1989, 155.

29 The Lollards, for example, had access to John Wycliffe's early translation of the Bible and were opposed to pilgrimage. They were active in England and Scotland during the 14th and 15th centuries.

30 Stranks, *This Sumptuous Church*, 3.

31 Sigal, *Marcheurs*, 45–7.

32 *The Enchiridion*, trans. Ford Lewis Battles, in *Advocates of Reform*, ed. Matthew Spinka, London, 1953, 337–8; *The Praise of Folly*, in John P. Dolan, *The Essential Erasmus*, London, 1964, 129–131.

33 Martin Luther, *Table Talk/Tischreden* 3588.

34 Opening lines from 'The Passionate Man's Pilgrimage', c.1603.

35 1 Sam.1.1–18.

36 Plinval, quoted in Sigal, *Marcheurs*, ibid.

37 Ian Reader and Tony Walker, *Pilgrimage in Popular Culture*, 6–16, discussing the ideas of Victor and Edith Turner.

38 *On Pilgrimage*, 208.

39 op. cit. xi.

40 Just one example: 'Concealed in the heart of all beings lies the Atman, the Spirit, the Self; smaller than the smallest atom, greater than the greatest spaces... I know that Spirit whose infinity is in all, who is ever one beyond time.' *Svetavatara Upanishad* 3.

41 *Interior Castle*, London, 1974, 6.

42 1 Corinthians 13, 13.

43 Mtt.16.24–25.

Resources

The resources in this section represent a personal choice and are offered only as suggestions or as a contribution to a wider whole. Many pilgrims bring prayers and readings of their own, reflecting their own styles and traditions. Some groups make up booklets of materials to carry with them. For those who are short of time, or who are uncertain about DIY liturgy from scratch, *A Wee Worship Book: Fourth Incarnation*, Wild Goose Publications, Glasgow, 1999, provides a basic framework without being either stuffy or trivialising. It is just one of the many recently-written collections of prayers and songs produced by the Iona Community and is available from most good religious bookshops, along with similar materials from other publishers.

Some of the men and women I spoke to in the course of writing this book could not imagine themselves praying out loud at any point during the walk. I suspect this would be the norm for most people in our culture today. Jesus himself had a distaste for public displays of piety, but he was talking to people who wanted to be admired for praying on street corners, not those of us who are simply shy or uncertain. Prayer has always been a traditional part of pilgrimage and in many parts of the world causes no embarrassment at all.

There are, of course, ways of praying which are quite invisible. I mention this not to provide a remedy for terminal shyness (though it can of course be used as such) but to put these resources into some kind of perspective. They are, at best, just the record, the afterglow, of other people's experiences. To experience what they are talking about for ourselves, there comes a time when we need to put away the books. If prayer is really 'a lifting of the mind and heart to God', then it can be far more than just readings and recitations. It can be an inner conversation, a way of seeing, a way of walking. It can happen alone or in company, with or without words.

Readings from Bede and the Anonymous Monk

Cuthbert and Boisil

At this time, Cuthbert was struck down by a plague which was ravaging the length and breadth of the country... The monks spent the whole night in prayer, for they felt they could not do without him on account of his holiness. His reply next morning when one of the monks mentioned the vigil – for they had kept it quiet from him – was: 'Then what am I lying here for? God will certainly have heard the prayers of so many good men. Fetch me my shoes and stick.' He got up there and then and tried to walk with the stick. Day by day his strength came back till he was quite recovered; only the swelling on the thigh seemed to move inwards, and for almost the whole of his life he was troubled with some internal pain, so that, to quote the apostle, 'strength was made perfect in weakness'.

Boisil saw that he was better and prophesied that he would never again be stricken by the same malady. 'At the same time,' said Boisil, 'I warn you not to lose the chance of learning from me, for death is upon me. By next week my body and voice shall have lost their strength.' Cuthbert knew that he was telling the truth. 'Then tell me what is the best book to study, one that can be got through in a week.'

'St John the Evangelist,' Boisil answered. 'I have a commentary in seven parts. With the help of God we can read one a day and perhaps discuss it if we want.'

It was done as he said. They were able to finish quickly because they dealt not with the profound arguments but with the simple things of 'the faith which worketh by love'. On the seventh day, when the reading was finished, illness overtook Boisil, and – this I recount with gladness – he entered into the joy of eternal bliss. He is believed to have unfolded all Cuthbert's future during that week. He was a prophet and a very holy man.

— *Bede, Life of Cuthbert 8*

Aidan and the king's horse

King Oswin had given Bishop Aidan a very fine horse, in order that he could ride whenever he had to cross a river or undertake any difficult or urgent journey, although the bishop ordinarily went on foot. Not long afterwards, when a poor man met the bishop and asked for alms, the bishop immediately dismounted and ordered the horse with all its royal trappings to be given to the beggar; for he was most compassionate, a protector of the poor and a father to the wretched. When this action came to the king's ears, he asked the bishop as they were going in to dine: 'My lord bishop, why did you give away the royal horse which was necessary for your own use? Have we not many less valuable horses and other belongings which would have been good enough for beggars, without giving away a horse that I had specially selected for your personal use?' The bishop at once answered, 'What are you saying, Your Majesty? Is this child of a mare more valuable to you than this child of God?' At this they went in to dinner, and the bishop sat down in his place; but the king, who had come in from hunting, stood warming himself by the fire with his attendants. As he stood by the fire, the king turned over in his mind what the bishop had said; then suddenly unbuckling his sword and handing it to a servant, he impulsively knelt at the bishop's feet and begged his forgiveness saying: 'I will not refer to the matter again, nor will I enquire how much of our bounty you have given away to God's children.'

— *Bede, Ecclesiastical History, III.14.*

Cuthbert and the sick child

Tydi, the priest whom I have mentioned, told me the following: 'Our holy bishop, during the plague which depopulated many places, was preaching the word of God to the people who survived in a certain village called Medilwong, when he turned to me and said gently: "Is there anyone in the village still suffering from that pestilence so that I may go forth and preach to him and bless him?" I pointed out to him a woman who was standing not far from us, weeping and wailing on account of her son who was lately dead, and holding another one in her arms, with his whole body swollen, half-dead and breathing his last. He straightway rose and approached her, and blessing the infant, kissed it, saying to the mother: "Woman, do not weep; your child will be saved and no one of all your household, who is still alive, will perish by the plague." And the mother and child who are still alive are witnesses of the truth of this.'

— *Anonymous, IV.vi*

Cuthbert, the boy and the eagle

On a certain day, he was going along the river Teviot and making his way southward, teaching the country people among the mountains and baptising them. Having a boy walking with him in his company, he said to him: 'Do you think that someone has prepared you your midday meal today?' He answered that he knew none of their kindred along that way and he did not hope for any sort of kindness from unknown strangers. The servant of God said again to him: 'My son, be of good cheer; the Lord will provide food for those who hope in him, for he said, "Seek ye first the Kingdom of God and his righteousness and all these things shall be added unto you," in order that the saying of the prophet may be fulfilled: "I have been young and now am old, yet have I not seen the righteous forsaken," and so forth. For the labourer is worthy of his hire.' After some such words he looked up to heaven and saw an eagle flying in the sky and said to his boy: 'This is the eagle which the Lord has instructed to provide us with food today.' After a short time, as they went on their way, they saw an eagle settling on the bank of the river. The boy ran towards the eagle in

accordance with the command of the servant of God, and stop-
ping, he found a large fish. The boy brought the whole of it to
him, whereupon Cuthbert said: 'Why did you not give our fisherman a part of it to eat since he was fasting?' Then the boy, in accordance with the commands of the man of God, gave half of the fish
to the eagle while they took the other half with them, and broiling
it in the company of some men, they ate it, and gave some to the
others and were satisfied, worshipping God and giving thanks.
Then they set out according to God's will to the mountains, as we
have said above, teaching and baptising people in the name of the
Father and of the Son and of the Holy Spirit.

—Anonymous, II.5

The healing of Eadswith

There was a sheriff of King Ecfrith, called Hildmer, a man dedicated to good works along with all his household and therefore
specially loved by Cuthbert. He visited Hildmer whenever he happened to be in the neighbourhood. His wife (Eadswith), though
zealous in almsgiving and all the other fruits of virtue, was suddenly possessed of a devil. She was so sorely vexed that she
would gnash her teeth and fling her arms and legs about. It was
terrifying to see or hear her. The convulsions gradually exhausted
her, and she was already at death's door, or so it seemed, when
her husband galloped off to fetch Cuthbert.

'My wife is ill,' he pleaded. 'She is very near her end. Send a
priest before she goes, to give her the body and blood of the Lord
and to bury her in holy ground.'

He was ashamed to admit that she whom Cuthbert was used
to seeing well was now out of her mind. Cuthbert went off to see
whom he could send when suddenly it came to him that she was
in the grip of no ordinary illness; she was possessed. He returned.

'I will not send anyone else. I ought to go back with you and
see her myself.'

As they were going along the sheriff began to weep. The bitterness of his anguish was apparent from the floods of tears. He
was afraid that when Cuthbert found she was mad he might think
she had served God up to now only in feigned faith. But the man

of God gently soothed his fears.

'Do not weep. Your wife's condition will not astonish me. I know, even though you are ashamed to admit it, that she is afflicted by a demon. I know too that before I arrive the demon will have left her and she herself will come running out to meet us as sound as ever. She will take the reins, bid us come in quickly and treat us with her usual attention. It is not only the wicked who are stricken down in this way. God, in his inscrutable designs, sometimes lets the innocent in this world be blighted by the devil, in mind as well as in body.' Cuthbert continued to console and instruct his friend in this vein, and as they approached the house the evil spirit, unable to bear the coming of the Holy Spirit with whom Cuthbert was filled, suddenly departed.

— *Bede's prose Life of Cuthbert 15*

Cuthbert and the otters

Cuthbert was sent for by the nun Aebbe, a widow, and the mother of them in Christ. He came to the monastery which is called Coldingham, in response to the invitation, and remaining there some days, did not relax his habitual way of life but began to walk about by night on the seashore, keeping up his custom of singing as he kept vigil. When a certain cleric of the community found this out, he began to follow him from a distance to test him, wishing to know what he did with himself at night. But that man of God, approaching the sea with mind made resolute, went into the waves up to his loin cloth; and once he was soaked as far as his armpits by the tumultuous and stormy sea. Then coming up out of the sea, he prayed, bending his knees on the sandy part of the shore, and immediately there followed in his footsteps two little sea animals, humbly prostrating themselves on the earth; and licking his feet, they rolled upon them, wiping them with their skins and warming them with their breath. After this service and ministry had been fulfilled and his blessing had been received, they departed to their haunts in the waves of the sea. But the man of God, returning home at cock-crow, came to the church of God to join in public prayer with the brethren. — *Anonymous, II.iii*

Songs, Hymns and Chants

This Day God Gives Me
(Tune: Morning has broken)

This day God gives me strength of high heaven
Sun and moon shining, flame in my hearth
Flashing of lightning
Wind in its swiftness, deeps of the ocean
Firmness of earth

This day God sends me
Strength as my steersman
Might to uphold me
Wisdom as guide
Your eyes are watchful
Your ears are listening
Your lips are speaking
Friend at my side

God's way is my way
God's shield is round me
God's host defends me
Saving from ill
Angel of heaven
Drive from me always
All that would harm me
Stand by me still.

Rising I thank you
Mighty and strong One
King of creation
Giver of rest
Firmly confessing
Threeness of Persons
Oneness of Godhead
Trinity blest.

*(Traditional Gaelic melody. Words by James Quinn,
based on 'St Patrick's Breastplate')*

A Touching Place
(Tune: Dream Angus)

Christ's is the world in which we move
Christ's are the folk we're summoned to love
Christ's is the voice that calls us to care
And Christ is the one who meets us here.

Chorus:
To the lost Christ shows his face
To the unloved he gives his embrace
To those who cry in pain or disgrace
Christ makes, with his friends, a touching place.

Feel for the people we most avoid
Strange or bereaved or never employed;
Feel for the women and feel for the men
Who fear that their living is all in vain.

Feel for the parents who've lost their child,
Feel for the women whom men have defiled
Feel for the baby for whom there's no breast
And feel for the weary who find no rest.

Feel for the lives by life confused,
Riddled with doubt, in loving abused;
Feel for the lonely heart conscious of sin,
Which longs to be pure but fears to begin.

Many and Great

mysteriously

Man - y and great, O God, are your works,

Ma - ker of earth and sky;

your hands have set the hea - vens with stars;

your fin - gers spread the moun - tains and plains.

You mere - ly spoke and wa - ters were formed;

deep seas o - bey your voice.

Many and great, O God, are your works,
Maker of earth and sky:
Your hands have set the heavens with stars;
Your fingers spread the mountains and plains.
You merely spoke and waters were formed;
Deep seas obey your voice.

Grant us communion with you, our God,
You who transcend the stars.
Come close to us and stay by our side:
With you are found the true gifts that last.
Grant us the life that never shall end,
Eternal life with you.

Dakota Indian Hymnal, paraphrased by Philip Frazier (1892–1964)
© 1916 Walton Music. Music: traditional.
Recording by the Wild Goose Worship Group.
'Many and Great: Songs of the World Church', Glasgow, 1990.

The Lord is My Shepherd

(Round)

The Lord is my shepherd, I'll trust in him always
He leads me by still waters, I'll trust in him always

Always, always, I'll trust in him always
Always, always, I'll trust in him always.

Kindle a Flame

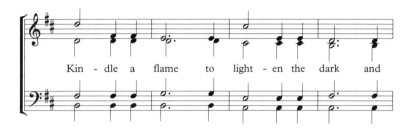

Kindle a flame
To lighten the dark
And take all fear away

*John L. Bell & Graham Maule, recorded by the Wild Goose Worship Group on
'Heaven Shall Not Wait', Glasgow, 1990.*

My Soul is Filled With Joy

(Tune: Will ye go, lassie, go?)

My soul is filled with joy
As I sing to God my Saviour
He has looked upon his servant
He has visited his people

Chorus:
And holy is his name
Through all generations
Everlasting is his mercy
To the people he has chosen
And holy is his name.

I am lowly as a child
But I know from this day forward
That my name will be remembered
And all people call me blessed

I proclaim the power of God
He does marvels for his servants
Though he scatters the proud-hearted
And destroys the might of princes

To the hungry he gives food
Sends the rich away empty
In his mercy he is mindful
Of the people he has chosen

In his love he now fulfils
What he promised to our forebears
I will praise the Lord, my Saviour
Everlasting is his mercy

(Words anon; based on the Magnificat. Lk.1.46–55)

Bless the Lord, My Soul

Bless the Lord, my soul, and bless God's ho - ly name. ___

Bless the Lord, my soul, who leads me in - to life.

Bless the Lord, my soul
And bless God's holy name
Bless the Lord, my soul
Who leads me into life

*(Music: J. Berthier © Ateliers et Presses de Taizé,
71250 Taizé-communauté, France)*

Guide Me, Oh Thou Great Redeemer

Guide me, O thou great Redeemer,
pilgrim through this barren land
I am weak, but thou art mighty,
hold me with thy powerful hand:
Bread of heaven, bread of heaven
Feed me till I want no more
Feed me till I want no more

Open now the crystal fountain, whence the healing stream doth
flow
Let the fire and cloudy pillar lead me all my journey through
Strong deliverer, strong deliverer
Be thou still my strength and shield
Be thou still my strength and shield.

When I tread the verge of Jordan, bid my anxious fears subside
Death of death and hell's destruction, land me safe on Canaan's
side
Songs of praises, songs of praises
I will ever give to thee
I will ever give to thee

(Original Welsh by Williams Pantycelyn trans. by Peter Williams)

Bible Readings

In the beginning (Genesis 1.1–31; 2.1–3 abridged)

In the beginning God created the heavens and the earth. The earth was without form and void, and darkness was upon the face of the deep; and the Spirit of God was moving over the face of the waters. And God said, 'Let there be light,' and there was light. And God saw that the light was good; and God separated the light from the darkness. God called the light Day, and the darkness he called Night. And there was evening and there was morning, one day.

And God said, 'Let there be a firmament in the midst of the waters and let it separate the waters from the waters'... And it was so. And God called the firmament Heaven. And there was evening and there was morning, a second day.

And God said, 'Let the waters under the heaven be gathered together into one place, and let the dry land appear.' And it was so. God called the dry land Earth, and the waters that were gathered together, he called Seas. And God saw that it was good. And God said, 'Let the earth put forth vegetation, plants yielding seed, and fruit trees bearing fruit in which is their seed, each according to their kind.' And it was so... And God saw that it was good. And there was evening and there was morning, a third day.

And God said, 'Let there be lights in the firmament of the heavens to separate the day from the night; and let them be for signs and for seasons and for days and years...' And it was so. And God made the two great lights, the greater light to rule the day, and the lesser light to rule the night; he made the stars also... And God saw that it was good. And there was evening and there was morning, a fourth day.

And God said, 'Let the waters bring forth swarms of living creatures, and let birds fly above the earth across the firmament of the heavens.' So God created the great sea monsters and every living creature that moves... And God saw that it was good. And God blessed them, saying, 'Be fruitful and multiply and fill the waters in the seas, and let birds multiply on the earth.' And there was evening and there was morning, a fifth day.

And God said, 'Let the earth bring forth living creatures according to their kinds; cattle and creeping things and beasts of the earth according to their kinds.' And it was so... And God saw that it was good.

Then God said, 'Let us make man in our image, after our likeness; and let them have dominion over the fish of the sea, and over the birds of the air, and over the cattle, and over all the earth... ' So God created man in his own image, in the image of God he created him; male and female he created them. And God blessed them, and God said to them, 'Be fruitful and multiply, and fill the earth and subdue it... And God said, 'Behold, I have given you every plant yielding seed which is upon the earth, and every tree with seed in its fruit; you shall have them for food. And to every beast of the earth, and to every bird of the air, and to everything that creeps on the earth, everything that has the breath of life, I have given every green plant for food.' And it was so. And God saw everything that he had made, and behold, it was very good. And there was evening and there was morning, a sixth day.

Thus the heavens and the earth were finished and all the host of them. And on the seventh day God finished his work which he had done, and he rested... So God blessed the seventh day, and hallowed it, because on it God rested from all his work which he had done in creation.

Praise of the Creator (from Psalm 104)

Bless the Lord, O my soul
O Lord my God, you are very great
You are clothed in honour and majesty;
wrapped in light as with a garment.
You stretch out the heavens like a tent,
You set the beams of your chambers on the waters,
You make the clouds your chariot,
You ride on the wings of the wind,
You make the winds your messengers
Fire and flame your ministers...
You make springs gush forth in the valleys,
They flow between the hills,
Giving drink to every wild animal;
The wild asses quench their thirst.

By the streams, the birds of the air have their habitation;
They sing among the branches.

Jacob's Dream (Genesis 28:10–17)

Jacob left Beer-sheba and went toward Haran. And he came to a certain place, and stayed there that night, because the sun had set. Taking one of the stones of the place, he put it under his head and lay down in that place to sleep. And he dreamed that there was a ladder set up on the earth, and the top of it reached to heaven; and behold, the angels of God were ascending and descending on it! And behold the Lord stood above it, and said, 'I am the Lord, the God of Abraham your father and the God of Isaac; the land on which you lie I will give to you and to your descendants; and your descendants shall be like the dust of the earth, and you shall be spread abroad to the west and to the east and to the north and to the south; and by you and your descendants shall all the families of the earth bless themselves. Behold, I am with you and will keep you wherever you go; for I will not leave you until you have done that of which I have spoken to you.' Then Jacob woke from his sleep and said, 'Surely the Lord is in this place; and I did not know it.' And he was afraid and said, 'How awesome is this place! This is none other than the house of God, and this is the gate of heaven.'

Prayer in time of distress (from Psalm 42)

As a deer longs for the flowing streams
So my soul longs for you, O God.
My soul thirsts for God, for the living God
When shall I come and behold the face of God?

My tears have been my food day and night
While people say to me continually,
'Where is your God?'

These things I remember as I pour out my soul:
How I went with the throng
And led them in processions to the house of God

With glad shouts and songs of thanksgiving
A multitude keeping festival.

Why are you cast down, O my soul,
And why are you disquieted within me?
Hope in God; for I shall again praise him,
My help and my God.

The Call of Samuel (1 Samuel 3.1–10)

Now the boy Samuel was ministering to the Lord under Eli. And the word of the Lord was rare in those days; there was no frequent vision. At that time, Eli, whose eyesight had begun to grow dim, so that he could not see, was lying down in his own place; the lamp of God had not yet gone down within the temple of the Lord, where the ark of God was. Then the Lord called, 'Samuel! Samuel!' and he said, 'Here I am!' and ran to Eli and said, 'Here I am, for you called me.' But he said, 'I did not call; lie down again.' So he went and lay down. And the Lord called again, 'Samuel!' And Samuel arose and went to Eli, and said, 'Here I am, for you called me.' But he said, 'I did not call, my son; lie down again.' Now Samuel did not yet know the Lord, and the word of God had not yet been revealed to him. And the Lord called Samuel again the third time. And he arose and went to Eli, and said, 'Here I am, for you called me.' Then Eli perceived that the Lord was calling the boy. Therefore Eli said to Samuel, 'Go, lie down; and if he calls you, you shall say, "Speak, Lord, for your servant hears."' So Samuel went and lay down in his place. And the Lord came and stood forth, calling as at other times, 'Samuel! Samuel!'. And Samuel said, 'Speak, for your servant hears.'

Survivor (from Psalm 40)

I waited, waited for the Lord
he bent down and heard my cry.
He brought me up out of the muddy pity,
out of the mire and the clay;
he set my feet on a rock
and gave me a firm footing;

and on my lips he put a new song,
a song of praise to our God.

True and false piety (Isaiah 58. 5–9)

Is such the fast that I choose, a day for a man to humble himself? Is it to bow down his head like a rush and spread sackcloth and ashes under him? Will you call this a fast, and a day acceptable to the Lord? Is this not the fast that I choose: to loose the bonds of wickedness; to undo the thongs of the yoke, to let the oppressed go free, and to break every yoke? Is it not to share your bread with the hungry, and bring the homeless poor into your house; when you see the naked, to cover him, and not to hide yourself from your own flesh? Then shall your light break forth like the dawn, and your healing shall spring up speedily; your righteousness shall go before you, the glory of the Lord shall be your rear guard. Then you shall call, and the Lord will answer; you shall cry, and he will say, Here I am.

The first commandment (Mark 12.28–33)

One of the scribes came up and... asked him, 'Which command-ment is the first of all?' Jesus answered, 'The first is, "Hear, O Israel: The Lord our God, the Lord is one; and you shall love the Lord your God with all your heart, and with all your soul, and with all your mind, and with all your strength." The second is this, "You shall love your neighbour as yourself." There is no other com-mandment greater than these'. And the scribe said to him, 'You are right, Teacher; you have truly said that he is one, and there is no other but he; and to love him with all the heart, and with all the strength, and to love one's neighbour as oneself, is much more than all whole burnt offerings and sacrifices.' And when Jesus saw that he answered wisely, he said to him, 'You are not far from the Kingdom of God.'

The Light of the World (Matthew 5.1–10, 13–16)

When Jesus saw the crowds, he went up the mountain; and after he had sat down his disciples came to him. Then he began to speak, and taught them, saying:
'Blessed are the poor in spirit, for theirs is the kingdom of heaven.

Blessed are the meek, for they will inherit the earth.

Blessed are those who hunger and thirst for righteousness, for they will be filled.

Blessed are the merciful, for they will receive mercy.

Blessed are the pure in heart, for they will see God.

Blessed are the peacemakers, for they will be called children of God.

Blessed are those who are persecuted for righteousness' sake, for theirs is the kingdom of heaven...

You are the salt of the earth; but if salt has lost its taste, how can its saltiness be restored? It is no longer good for anything, but is thrown out and trampled underfoot. You are the light of the world. A city built on a hill cannot be hid. No one, after lighting a lamp, puts it under the bushel basket, but on the lampstand, and it gives light to all the house. In the same way, let your light shine before others, so that they may see your good works and give glory to your Father in heaven.'

Mercy not sacrifice (Matthew 9. 9–13)

As Jesus was walking along, he saw a man called Matthew sitting at the tax booth; and he said to him, 'Follow me.' And he got up and followed him. And as he sat at dinner in the house, many tax collectors and sinners came and were sitting with him and his disciples. When the Pharisees saw this, they said to his disciples, 'Why does your teacher eat with tax collectors and sinners?' But when he heard this, he said, 'Those who are well have no need of a physician, but those who are sick. Go and learn what this means: "I desire mercy, not sacrifice." For I have come not to call the righteous but sinners'.

Fellow-travellers (Luke 9.49)

John said 'Master, we saw someone casting out demons in your name, and we tried to stop him, because he does not follow with us.' But Jesus said to him, 'Do not stop him; for whoever is not against you is for you.'

The greatest people (Matthew 18.1–6, 10–11)
At that time the disciples came to Jesus and asked, 'Who is the greatest in the kingdom of heaven?' He called a child, whom he put among them, and said, 'Truly I tell you, unless you change and become like children you will never enter the kingdom of heaven. Whoever becomes humble like this child is the greatest in the kingdom of heaven. Whoever welcomes one such child in my name welcomes me. If any of you put a stumbling block before one of these little ones who believe in me, it would be better for you if a great millstone were fastened around your neck and you were drowned in the depths of the sea... Take care that you do not despise one of these little ones; for I tell you, in heaven their angels continually see the face of my Father in heaven.'

Two parables of the kingdom (Luke 13.18–20)
He said therefore, 'What is the kingdom of God like? And to what should I compare it? It is like a mustard seed that someone took and sowed in the garden; it grew and became a tree, and the birds of the air made nests in its branches.' And again he said, 'To what should I compare the kingdom of God? It is like yeast that a woman took and mixed in with three measures of flour until all of it was leavened.'

Jesus washes his disciples' feet (John 13.1–15)
Now before the festival of the Passover, Jesus knew that his hour had come to depart from this world and go to the Father. Having loved his own who were in the world, he loved them to the end. The devil had already put it into the heart of Judas son of Simon Iscariot to betray him. And during supper, Jesus, knowing that the Father had given all things into his hands, and that he had come from God and was going to God, got up from the table, took off his outer robe, and tied a towel around himself. Then he poured water into a basin and began to wash the disciples' feet and to wipe them with the towel that was tied around him. He came to Simon Peter, who said to him, 'Lord, are you going to wash my feet?' Jesus answered, 'You do not know now what I am doing, but later you will understand.' Peter said to him, 'You will never wash my feet.' Jesus answered, 'Unless I wash you, you have no share

with me.' Simon Peter said to him, 'Lord, not my feet only but also my hands and my head!' Jesus said to him, 'One who has bathed does not need to wash, except for the feet, but is entirely clean. And you are clean, though not all of you'. For he knew who was to betray him; for this reason he said, 'Not all of you are clean.'

After he had washed their feet, had put on his robe, and had returned to the table, he said to them, 'Do you know what I have done for you? You call me Teacher and Lord – and you are right, for that is what I am. So if I, your Lord and Teacher, have washed your feet, you also ought to wash one another's feet. For I have set you an example, that you also should do as I have done to you.'

The first Easter (Luke 24.13–35)

Now on that same day two of them were going to a village called Emmaus, about seven miles from Jerusalem, and talking to each other about all these things that had happened. While they were talking and discussing, Jesus himself came near and went with them, but their eyes were kept from recognising him. And he said to them, 'What are you discussing with each other while you walk along?' They stood still, looking sad. Then one of them, whose name was Cleopas, answered him. 'Are you the only stranger in Jerusalem who does not know the things that have taken place there in these days?' He asked them, 'What things?' They replied, 'The things about Jesus of Nazareth, who was a prophet mighty in deed and word before God and all the people, and how our chief priests and leaders handed him over to be condemned to death and crucified him. But we had hoped that he was the one to redeem Israel. Yes, and besides this, it is now the third day since these things took place. Moreover, some women of our group astounded us. They were at the tomb early this morning, and when they did not find his body there, they came back and told us that they had indeed seen a vision of angels who said he was alive. Some of those who were with us went to the tomb and found it just as the women had said; but they did not see him.' Then he said to them, 'Oh how foolish you are, and how slow of heart to believe all that the prophets have declared! Was it not necessary that the Messiah should suffer these things and then enter into his glory?' Then, beginning with Moses and all the prophets, he interpreted to them the things about himself in all the scriptures.

As they came near to the village to which they were going, he walked ahead as if he were going on. But they urged him strongly, saying, 'Stay with us, because it is almost evening and the day is now nearly over.' So he went in to stay with them. When he was at the table with them, he took bread, blessed and broke it, and gave it to them. Then their eyes were opened, and they recognised him; and he vanished from their sight. They said to each other, 'Were not our hearts burning within us while he was talking to us on the road, while he was opening the scriptures to us?' That same hour, they got up and returned to Jerusalem; and they found the eleven and their companions gathered together. They were saying, 'The Lord has risen indeed, and he has appeared to Simon.' Then they told what had happened on the road, and how he had been made known to them in the breaking of bread.

Clothe yourselves with compassion (Colossians 3.12)

As God's chosen ones, holy and beloved, clothe yourselves with compassion, kindness, humility, meekness and patience. Bear with one another and, if anyone has a complaint against another, forgive each other; just as the Lord has forgiven you, so you also must forgive. Above all, clothe yourselves with love, which binds everything together in perfect harmony. And let the peace of Christ rule in your hearts.

Everyone who loves is a child of God (1 John 4.7–12)

Dear friends, let us love one another, because love is from God; everyone who loves is a child of God and knows God, but the unloving know nothing of God. For God is love; and his love was disclosed to us in this, that he sent his only Son into the world to bring us life. The love I speak of is not our love for God, but the love he has shown us in sending his Son as the remedy for our sins. If God thus loved us, dear friends, we in turn are bound to love one another. Though God has never been seen by anyone, if we love one another, God dwells in us and his love is brought to perfection within us.

Prayers, Poems & other Readings

Pilgrimage prayer

Open our eyes, Lord, to see your glory;
Open our ears to hear your call;
Open our lips to sing your praises.
Then guide us on our pilgrimage of faith,
That with the memory of Cuthbert in our hearts
We may walk with him who is
The way, the truth and the life,
And find our freedom in your service
Through Jesus Christ
Amen

– Prayer from Durham Cathedral (adapted)

Blessing of the Pilgrimage

Bless, O God, the earth beneath my feet,
Bless, O God, the road that I must take
Bless, O God, the purpose that I seek
O God of gods
Your blessing on my rest.

Bless my desire
Bless my intention
Bless my hope
O King of kings
Your blessing on my sight

— Alexander Carmichael, Carmina Gadelica III, 181

Invocation

Creator of rainbows
Come through the closed doors
Of our emotions, mind and imagination;
Come alongside us as we walk
Come and call us by name
Call us to pilgrimage

— Kate McIlhagga, Encompassing Presence

Bede's prayer
Lord, you have let me drink
At the well of your teaching.
Fountain of all Wisdom
let me come to you at last
To be in your presence for ever.

— *(Ecclesiastical History, closing prayer)*

Wrapped in love I saw that God is everything which is good and comforting for our help. He is our clothing, for he is that love which wraps and enfolds us, embraces us and guides us, surrounds us for his love, which is so tender that he may never desert us. And so in this sight I saw truly that he is everything which is good, as I understand.

— *Julian of Norwich (1342–1423), Showings 4*

Benediction
When words are done
We speak in silences:
When strength is gone
We find our strength in these

These are the hands
Which are the heart's all-heal:
Memory of friends
And the earth's 'Be still'.

Nothing is ours;
Yet silences begin
To open doors
By which life enters in.

– *William Soutar, Poems in Scots and English*
ed. W.R. Aitken, Edinburgh & London, 1975, 33

Benediction of a day

There is a living flower. You want to have it, so you pluck it. But, by your act of plucking it, it dies. You are fascinated by a sparkling running stream, a living stream of water. But, as you grasp it, it runs through your fingers, you scoop it into a pail, you no longer have life, just a a bucket of H_2O. There is a sunbeam dancing in your room. If you pull down the curtain to capture the beam, it is gone. There is a bracing wind that enlivens your whole being. But try to catch it in a bag and you have stagnant air. All this reminds us how not to get in touch with life. Here is the root trouble of our lives. We all love life, but the moment we try to hold it, we miss it. The fact that things change and move and flow is their life. Try to make them static and you die of worry.

This is just as true of God who is the Life of life. The only way to achieve a sense of God's presence is to put yourself in the way of Him. In our analogy, you achieve a sense of life in the presence of a flower, by a running stream, in a bracing wind, with sunbeams falling on the stream. You come home to say you have had a perfectly lovely day, which means a lively day. It has been a benediction of a day. You can only achieve a sense of God in a similar way... You can only find God in the now.

—George McLeod, Sermon on Prayer, July 1955.

The hard road

To come to the knowledge you have not
you must go by a way in which you know not
To come to the possession you have not
you must go by a way in which you possess not
To come to be what you are not
you must go by a way in which you are not...
In this nakedness the spirit finds
its quietude and rest.
For in coveting nothing, nothing raises it up
and nothing weighs it down,
because it is in the centre of its humility.

— St John of the Cross, from The Ascent of Mount Carmel,
13 Collected Works ed. Kieran Kavanaugh and Otilio Rodriguez,
Washington, 1979, 104.

Readings from Non-Christian Traditions

Invitation

Come, come, whoever you are
Wanderer, fire-worshipper, lover of leaving
Ours is not a caravan of despair
Even if you have broken your promise a thousand times
Come, come again, come.

— *Mevlana Jelalud'din Rumi*

Grace of seeing

May God, who in the mystery of his vision and power transforms his white radiance into his many-coloured creation, from whom all things come and into whom they all return, grant us the grace of pure vision.

— *Svetasvatara Upanishad 4.*

Starlight and Non-Being

Starlight asked Non-Being: 'Master, are you? Or are you not?' Since he received no answer whatever, Starlight set himself to watch for Non-Being. He waited to see if Non-Being would put in an appearance. He kept his eyes fixed on the deep Void, hoping to catch a glimpse of Non-Being. All day long he looked, and he saw nothing. He listened, but heard nothing. He reached out to grasp, and grasped nothing.

Then Starlight exclaimed at last: 'This is IT!
This is the furthest yet! Who can reach it?
I can comprehend the absence of Being
But who can comprehend the absence of Nothing?
If now, on top of all this, Non-Being IS,
Who can comprehend it?'

— *The Way of Chuang Tzu, xxii.8, Thomas Merton.*

Shine
Like the moon,
Come out from behind the clouds
Shine.

— Dhammapada 25

Abbreviations

Anon. Anonymous *Life of Cuthbert*.

BB *The Borders Book*, Donald Omand (ed.), Edinburgh, 1995.

CCC *St Cuthbert: his Cult and his Community*, Gerald Bonner, David Rollason and Clare Stancliffe (eds) Woodbridge, 1989.

DSCHT *Dictionary of Scottish Church History and Theology*, Nigel M. de S. Cameron, David F. Wright, David C. Lachman and Donald E. Meek (eds), Edinburgh, 1993.

EH Bede, *Ecclesiastical History of the English People*.

HBNS *History of the Berwickshire Naturalists' Society*.

Life Bede's Prose *Life of Cuthbert*.

LL James Fleming Leishman, *Linton Leaves*, Edinburgh, 1937.

Further Reading

Primary sources

Bede, *Ecclesiastical History of the English People*, Penguin Classics, 1990.

Bede, *Life of Cuthbert*, in *The Age of Bede*, ed. D.H. Farmer, Penguin Classics, 1988.

Anonymous *Life of Cuthbert*, in *Two Lives of St Cuthbert*, ed. Bertram Colgrave, Cambridge University Press, 1940.

Secondary material

David Adam, *Fire of the North*, London, 1993.

Janet Backhouse, *The Lindisfarne Gospels*, Oxford, 1981.

Gerald Bonner, David Rollason and Claire Stancliffe (eds), *St Cuthbert, his Cult and his Community*, Woodbridge, 1989.

E. Patricia Dennison and Russell Coleman, *Historic Melrose*, Edinburgh, 1998.

Jane Hawkes, *The Golden Age of Northumbria*, Newcastle, 1996

Jennifer Lash, *On Pilgrimage*, London, 1998.

Henry Meyr-Harting, *The Coming of Christianity to Anglo-Saxon England*, revised edition, London, 1991.

Martin Robinson, *An Anthology of Pilgrimage*, London, 1998.

Clare Stancliffe, 'Cuthbert and the Polarity between Pastor and Solitary', in *St Cuthbert*, above, pp. 21–44.

Benedicta Ward, 'The Spirituality of St Cuthbert' in *St Cuthbert* above pp. 65–76, and also available as a booklet from Fairacres Publications, Oxford.

Peter Yeoman, *Pilgrimage in Medieval Scotland*, Edinburgh, 1999.

Acknowledgements

To Cambridge University Press for extracts from the Anonymous *Life of Cuthbert*, ed. Bertram Colgrave, in *Two Lives of St Cuthbert*, 1940; to John Bell and Graham Maule for the songs 'A Touching Place' and 'Kindle a Flame'; to Dick Gaughan for the refrain from 'Both Sides the Tweed'; to the Trustees of the National Library of Scotland for William Soutar's poem 'Benediction'; to Ian McFadyen for his poem 'Arrival'; to Kate McIlhagga for 'Creator of Rainbows'. To Paulist Press for the extract from *Showings* by Julian of Norwich, translated by Edmund Colledge and James Walsh, New York, 1978; to the Washington Province of Discalced Carmelites, ICS Publications, 2131 Lincoln Road NE, Washington, D. 20002-1199, USA for the extract from 'The Ascent of Carmel' from *The Collected Works of St John of the Cross*, translated by Kieran Kavanagh and Otilio Rodriguez © 1979, 1991. To Penguin Books for permission to quote from Bede's Prose *Life of Cuthbert* in *The Age of Bede*, translated by J.F. Webb and edited by D.H. Farmer, London, 1965; from *Bede: Ecclesiastical History of the English People*, translated by Leo Sherley-Price, revised R.E. Latham, London, 1990; and from *The Upanishads*, translated by Juan Mascaro, Harmondsworth, 1965; to J. Berthier and the Ateliers et Presses de Taizé, 71250 Taizé-communauté, France, for the song 'Bless the Lord, My Soul'; to Geoffrey Chapman, a Cassell imprint, for 'This Day God Gives Me' by James Quinn; to HarperCollins Publishers Ltd for 'Come, come whoever you are' by Mevlana Jelalud'din Rumi, translated by R.A. Nicholson in *Rumi, Poet and Mystic*. The Cuthbert pilrimage prayer is reproduced with permission from the Dean and Chapter of Durham. 'Starlight and Non-Being' by Thomas Merton, from *The Way of Chuang Tzu*, © The Abbey of Gethsemane, is reprinted by permission of New Directions Publishing Corp. and Laurence Pollinger Ltd. To any copyright holder whose whereabouts I have been unable to trace, please accept my apologies and write to me c/o Wild Goose Publications. All biblical quotations are from the New Revised Standard Version of the Bible except Gen. 1–2.3, Gen. 28.10–17, 1 Samuel 3.1–10, Mk. 12.28–33 and Is. 58.5–9. These are quoted from the Common Bible and 1 John 4.7–12 and Ps. 40.1–3 from the New English Bible.

Thanks

I am very grateful to the following people who took the time to read and comment on parts of the manuscript: Ros and Ruth Anderson, Chris Badenoch, Professor Gerald Bonner, Professor Stuart Brown, Jane Dawson, John Dent, Dom Mark Dilworth, Bill Lonie, Revd Andrew Ross, Cliff Sharpe and friends, Professor T.C. Smout, Revd Kate Tristram and Vic Tokely. None of them read the manuscript in its entirety and I am solely responsible for any mistakes or errors of judgement.

Thank you also to the many friends and contacts who pointed me in the direction of information or provided much-needed corrections and challenges. It seems invidious to pick out anyone in particular, but the following really deserve a special mention: David Adam, Nils Blyth, Colin Clark, Walter Elliott, Maria Luz, Rory McDonald, Donald McGlynn, Larry Meyer, John Robinson, Ron Shaw, Roger Smith and the staff of St Mary's Mill, Selkirk. As ever, my greatest debt is to Bruce, without whom none of this would have been possible.

Index

The modern spelling of Anglo-Saxon names varies with different translators. Thus, 'd' and 'th' are often used interchangeably, Ebba and Aebbe are the same person, as are Oswy and Oswiu, but not Oswin. In general I have opted for simplicity – and shameless inconsistency, so if you don't find what you are looking for under one spelling, try another.

Gattonside 55
Gaughan, Dick 91
Gefrin 127–129
geese
  greylag 121
  pale-bellied brent 156
Genereus 31
George 105
Germanus 163
Gilry, John 110, 117
Girthgate 53
Glasgow 21, 55, 100
Glastonbury 173
Glen Road 74, 76
Glen, River 129, 131
Glendale 131
Gleneagles 122
goats 128
Gordon Moss 71
Gospels 76, 88, 136, 162, 164, 170
Grahams 90
Gregory the Great 125
Grendel 105
'Guide Me, Oh Thou Great
  Redeemer' 192
Gypsies 15, 81, 111–118

Haddington 118, 147
Halter Burn 119, 121
Hannah, mother of Samuel 174
Hare Craig 80
Harestanes 20, 85, 91, 95
Hawick 14, 69, 71, 74, 85, 96–97
hawks 56
hazelnuts 125
Heavenfield 32
Helena, Empress 162
Henry I 89
Henry VIII 90
Hereberht 47
Herefrith 48, 61
herring 151
Hethpool 124–125, 127
Hexham 32, 47, 123
hi-jeanies 81

Highland Clearances 74
Hilda 33, 37–38, 120
Hildmer 36, 51, 65, 83, 182
hillfort 128
'Holy Fairs' 102, 107
Holy Island (Lindisfarne) 16, 20, 24,
  25, 49, 133, 140, 149, 156
Holy Island (off Arran) 45
Holy Spirit 82, 103, 122–123,
  182–183
horse 27, 29–30, 65, 67, 81–82, 91,
  95, 104–105, 117, 140, 180
Hoselaw 121
  Hoselaw chapel 106
Hownam 103, 109–110
Hruringaham 29, 136
Hume, Peter 112
Humes 90
Hunter, John 109–110

Inner Farne 42–45, 49, 140–143, 155
Inquisition 165
Iona 27–28, 31–35, 37–40, 48, 62,
  79, 140, 143, 154, 162, 165–166,
  168, 173
Iona Community 106, 122, 173, 178
Iurminburg 47, 120

Jacob 111, 195
Jacobite 91
James, epistle writer 106
James I 147
James IV 114, 135
James VI and I 91, 99, 117
Jarrow 46, 52, 62, 163
Jedburgh 19–21, 91, 117
Jekyll, Gertrude 156
Jerome 162
Jerusalem 55, 57, 111, 159, 168, 176,
  200–201
Jesus 14, 28, 33, 38, 47, 49, 62, 76,
  87, 106, 111, 124, 136–137, 143,
  149–150, 159, 161–162, 164, 169,
  171, 175, 178, 197–200

Access assessment form: St Cuthbert's Way

(tick as required)

Location of site, e.g. Melrose Abbey			
Parking: reserved spaces	unreserved (close) 1	unreserved (distant) 2	unpredictable (e.g. can get busy)
Steps none	1–3	4–10	more than 10
Gradient level	slight	moderate	steep
Viewpoints (sitting position)	clear		obstructed
Passing places	yes		no

Seats (how many)	yes	no	seasonal	height

Distance (to and from main attraction)				
Surface hard and smooth	gravel	smooth grass	uneven	
Toilets dedicated	assisted	normal	none	

Inaccessible areas

Any other hazards?

Any special features/good points?

1 Close = within approx. 50 yds of entrance
2 Distant = more than 50 yds from entrance

Wild Goose Publications is part of

The Iona Community

The Iona Community is an ecumenical Christian community, founded in 1938 by the late Lord MacLeod of Fuinary (the Revd George MacLeod DD) and committed to seeking new ways of living the Gospel in today's world. Gathered around the rebuilding of the ancient monastic buildings of Iona Abbey, but with its original inspiration in the poorest areas of Glasgow during the Depression, the Community has sought ever since the 'rebuilding of the common life', bringing together work and worship, prayer and politics, the sacred and the secular in ways that reflect its strongly incarnational theology.

The Community today is a movement of over 200 Members, around 1,500 Associate Members and about 700 Friends. The Members – women and men from many backgrounds and denominations, most in Britain, but some overseas – are committed to a rule of daily prayer and Bible reading, sharing and accounting for their use of time and money, regular meeting and action for justice and peace.

The Iona Community maintains three centres on Iona and Mull: Iona Abbey and the MacLeod Centre on Iona, and Camas Adventure Camp on the Ross of Mull. Its base is in Community House, Glasgow, where it also supports work with young people, the Wild Goose Resource and Worship Groups, a bimonthly magazine (Coracle) and a publishing house (Wild Goose Publications).

For further information on the Iona Community please contact:

The Iona Community
Pearce Institute,
840 Govan Road
Glasgow G51 3UU
T. 0141 445 4561; F. 0141 445 4295
e-mail: ionacomm@gla.iona.org.uk